REVERSIBLE READINGS

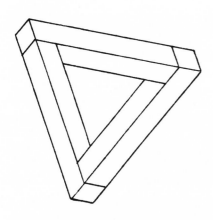

REVERSIBLE READINGS

Ambiguity in Four

Modern Latin American

Novels

PAUL B. DIXON

The University of Alabama Press

Publication of this book was made possible, in part, by financial
assistance from the Andrew W. Mellon Foundation and the American
Council of Learned Societies.

Permission to use copyrighted material is gratefully acknowledged to publishers and
authors as follows:

Passages from *Obras completas* by Machado de Assis. Copyright © 1959 by Editora
Nova Aguilar S/A. Used by permission.

Passages from *Pedro Páramo* by Juan Rulfo. Copyright © 1964 by Fondo de Cultura
Económica. Used by permission.

Passages from *Cien años de soledad* by Gabriel García Márquez. Copyright © 1971
by Editorial Sudamericana. Used by permission.

Passages from *Grande sertão: veredas* by João Guimarães Rosa. Copyright © 1984
by Editora Nova Fronteira S/A. Used by permission.

Passages from *The Concept of Ambiguity—the Example of James* by Shlomith Rimmon. Copyright © 1977 by the University of Chicago Press. Used by permission.

An illustration from "Impossible Objects: A Special Type of Visual Illusion," by L. S.
Penrose and R. Penrose, in *British Journal of Psychology*, 49. Copyright © 1958 by the
British Psychological Society. Used by permission.

to Barbara

Contents

Acknowledgments   ix

Preface   xi
1: **Ambiguity in Artistic Expression**   3
   Coexisting Mutually Exclusives / 5
   Types of Exclusive Propositions / 8
   The Ambiguity of "Ambiguity" / 9
   Other Expressions, Polysemic but Unambiguous / 13
   Ambiguity's Effects on the Reader / 20

2: *Dom Casmurro* as **Undertow**   23
   Ambiguity and Underlying Structures / 26
   Critics and the Novel's Ambiguity / 28
   A Mechanism of Ambiguity / 29
   A System of Clues / 33
   The Role of Point of View / 43
   Ambiguity as a Binder of Motifs / 45
   Metaphor and Universal Themes / 46
   A Metaliterary Reading / 51

3: **Three Versions of** *Pedro Páramo*   60
   The Near-solid Narrative Structure / 63
   The Expressionistic Reading / 74
   The Structure of Chiasmus / 82

4: *Cien años de soledad*'s **Unending End**   89
   Three Incompatible Facts / 91
   The Ending and the Critics / 97
   How the Novel Defines Itself / 101
      Readers in Macondo / 102
      The Short Circuit / 105
      Objects with No Nexus / 108

Self-destruction, Self-reconstruction / 109
Abrupt Reversals / 111
Solipsistic Encounters / 113
Repetition and Return / 114
The Problem of Tone / 119

5: **Transverse and Universe in *Grande sertão: veredas*** 125
Transparent and Opaque Language / 126
Axes and Crosscurrents / 136
The Disjunction in "Travessia" / 140

Epilogue 151

Notes 157

Bibliography 174

Index 183

Illustrations

Fig. 1.1 The Penrose "impossible object" 2
Fig. 1.2 Winson's Indian/Eskimo figure 4
Fig. 1.3 An ambiguous folded paper 19
Fig. 3.1 Rubin's "reversible goblet" 61
Fig. 4.1 The novel's impossible triad 95
Fig. 4.2 The "impossible object" made possible 96
Fig. 4.3 Reader-supplied connections 101

Acknowledgments

I wish to express gratitude to my wife, Barbara, for her patience and support during the course of this project, and for her helpful suggestions on the manuscript. I am also indebted to my parents and parents-in-law, Dr. and Mrs. Dwight R. Dixon and Dr. and Mrs. Edward L. Hart, for their continual confidence and assistance.

This book is a revised version of my doctoral thesis, from the University of North Carolina. For their attentive reading and valuable suggestions with the original version, special thanks to my adviser, Professor Fred Clark, and to Professors Lawrence A. Sharpe, María A. Salgado, Paul Borgeson, and Sima Godfrey. I particularly appreciate the efforts of Professor Sharpe in painstakingly reading the final version of the thesis, and those of Mrs. Billie Cozart in ways too numerous to mention.

Finally, I acknowledge the generous assistance of various individuals at the Biblioteca Julio Jiménez Rueda, part of the Centro de Estudios Literarios of the Universidad Nacional Autónoma de México, who provided me with research materials on Juan Rulfo.

Preface

This book is a study of four well-known Latin American novels. The first and last I will examine are Brazilian works: *Dom Casmurro* (1900) by Machado de Assis and *Grande sertão: veredas* (1956) by João Guimarães Rosa. Framed between these chapters on Portuguese-language novels are essays on two works in Spanish: *Pedro Páramo* (1955) by the Mexican Juan Rulfo, and *Cien años de soledad* (1967) by the Colombian Gabriel García Márquez.

In choosing these novels I wish to avoid giving the impression of being an ambitious David challenging not one, but four Goliaths. May I say that my stance before the works is more one of veneration than of challenge. I do not share the view of some contemporaries that criticism should be in competition with the literary text.[1] Instead, I hold to the rather traditional position that the work of art is a privileged expression, and that the role of criticism with respect to the work is one of support and cooperation.[2]

I have chosen the novels mentioned for a couple of reasons. The selection of works that have achieved the status of classics in Latin American literature—both Brazilian and Spanish-American—was determined partly by my desire to communicate to a broad audience of Latin Americanists upon familiar territory. Moreover, I selected these particular works because each illustrates in a different way the specific concept of ambiguity with which I am working. My treatment of the novels will thus build a series of variations on a single theme. Numerous Latin American novels may be called ambiguous in the broad sense of multivalent, unclear, or enigmatic. Many in fact may appear to be more significantly ambiguous in this sense than the novels I have chosen. However, the concept of ambiguity to be developed here—involving mutually exclusive, reversible readings—is more narrowly focused than in most studies. We find that many of the novels considered ambiguous in the broad sense do not qualify so well under our more narrow definition. When I speak of a selection of novels, therefore, I refer to a choice of works that hold in common certain distinctive features, and not simply to a random sampling. The class of ambiguous novels (by my definition) amounts to a kind of structurally determined genre, analogous to Todorov's genre of the fantastic.[3]

It may seem odd to some that I have included a novel published in 1900 with three produced around the middle of the century. Most readers familiar with Machado de Assis, however, realize that he is rather an anachronism in Latin American literature, and that it may be easier to group him with contemporary authors than with those belonging to the naturalistic or realistic schools around the turn of the century.[4]

Ambiguity has become one of the central concerns of contemporary criticism. What started as a pawn for the Anglo-American new critics has become queen for the structuralists, and practically the whole chess game for the poststructuralists. My study represents a modest attempt to take into account some of the statements of these contemporary schools of criticism. I have occasionally borrowed techniques, such as using a linguistic analogy to analyze narrative, employing Jakobson's metaphor/metonomy opposition to discuss opposing tendencies in some types of language, and exploring contradictory definitions or etymologies for certain words. However, I should point out that in some fundamental respects the study differs from the approach taken by these schools.

In a recent essay, Jonathan Culler discusses the debate taking place in America between the more traditional critics whose origins are in Anglo-American new criticism, and the more avant-garde critics, influenced by the continental schools of structuralism and deconstruction.[5] Probably there is not so clear a distinction between the schools, or so great a uniformity within them, as Culler's essay would suggest. Nevertheless, some generalizing is appropriate. On the four points of argument he outlines, I believe that this book tends to belong more to the camp of the old new critics:

(1) The Task of Criticism. According to Culler, the continental schools call for an explanation of the "uncanny logic that operates in texts whatever they say" (p. 3), a concentration upon a "science of literature, interested in the conditions of meaning" (p. 6), a deemphasis of individual works, and an emphasis on their underlying system.[6] The more traditional critics, on the other hand, still believe that "the task of criticism is to interpret literary works" (p. 3). While this book advances some theories about how ambiguous texts operate, I am not at all sure that the principles constitute a "science of literature" in general. On the other hand, I am confident that I do provide an interpretation of specific properties common to four individual works, based on a sufficient theoretical framework.

(2) The Question of Metalanguage. Culler attributes to the more traditional faction the acceptance of metalanguage, whether in criticism or in literary works, a language referring to a prior, original statement. In contrast, avant-garde criticism casts doubt on the distinction between criticism as a deferential metalanguage and original literary utterances. Concerning metalinguistic utterances in literature itself, he says, "A great deal of modern criticism has consisted of readings that question the authority previously granted to metalinguistic statements within works. We have learned that we need not believe a text when it tells us just what it means or how it functions" (p. 9). Here again, this book tends to fit the more traditional pattern. In each interpretive chapter, I discover that the work in some

fashion describes its own ambiguity. While I do not think this discovery constitutes "belief in the text when it tells us . . . how it functions" (how do we "take" a text that seems to describe explicitly its own indeterminacy?), I must acknowledge that I cast no doubt on the validity of metalanguage itself.

(3) The Problem of Referentiality. Avant-garde theories rest on the "denial that a work has a particular referent or is the assertion of a particular proposition" (p. 11), while more traditional ones continue to embrace the referentiality of literature. To attempt to associate this study with the former position would be to contradict its theoretical foundations. As chapter 1 shows, the very definition of ambiguity depends on the concept of "propositions"[7] and "meanings" underlying a work's utterances. As I just mentioned, the study accepts the notion of metalanguage. This implies the acceptance of referentiality, because metalanguage by definition is referential.

(4) The Problem of Determinacy of Indeterminacy of Meaning. While traditional critics posit determinacy of meaning, poststructuralists and many structuralists[8] posit "certain inescapable metaphysical oppositions" (p. 15) and plays of "undecidables" (p. 16). Obviously, "undecidables" are the eventual outcome of my study. However, I find it unnecessary to postulate this from the outset. Rather than proceeding from an assumption ab initio of indeterminacy for all written texts, as is the case with much current criticism, I begin by postulating the possibility of univocal meaning, perceived by the reader as a "finalized hypothesis." In the case of these specific novels, however, not one, but two or three *incompatible* finalized hypotheses are suggested. This causes an acknowledgment of the undecidability of these texts. But curiously, once we have made this acknowledgment, we find in the form of metaliterary language the description within the works of this very ambiguity. We are ultimately placed in the odd position of reading works that appear to determine their own indeterminacy. Failure to

achieve determinate meaning becomes, paradoxically, the overriding meaning of the works. Consequently, the very question of the determinacy or indeterminacy of written language is left undecidable for the novels in question. Rather than resolving the question in terms of some inevitable result of the tentative status of writing, the method leaves it an open question, to be asked by each reader for each individual work.

The novels selected illuminate a theory, but at the same time, I hope, the theory exposed here will help illuminate the novels. It is my desire that this book serve both deductively and inductively, that is, as a means for understanding specific works, and as a means for understanding generalities about art.

An outstanding feature of Latin American literature in general has been its cultivation of ambiguity, its revelry in pluralism of all sorts, and its tendency toward cryptic expression. This is particularly true of the modern Latin American novel, which according to Carlos Fuentes has ambiguity as one of its essential properties.[9] This may be a reflection of Latin America's tremendous cultural plurality, a consequence of its rather convoluted, difficult history, a desire to revolt against the status quo through revolutionary expression, an embrace of the overall tendencies of modern world literature, or of course a combination of these factors. In any case, it has been said that Latin American literature as a whole is abidingly baroque.[10] This book examines a specific manifestation of this more general phenomenon, focusing upon expressions that are reversible, or that prompt in the reader mutually exclusive hypotheses. I treat the novels as case studies of this phenomenon, and make very little effort to compare them with each other, or to relate them to a context. Those familiar with Latin American literature will realize, however, that the phenomenon of reversible interpretations is by no means anomalous.

A considerable body of criticism exists on each of the authors involved in this study. Practicality demands some limitations in taking these studies into account. Consequently, readers will not find references here to interpretive works (1) that do not specifically treat the novels in question and (2) that do not have some direct bearing on the manifestation of ambiguity as I discuss it. I recognize that some of the very important studies—such as Mattoso Câmara's work on Machado, Merrell's on Rulfo, Ludmer's on García Márquez, and some of Cavalcanti Proença's on Guimarães Rosa—remain unmentioned. But it is my hope that what I sacrifice in comprehensiveness I will gain in depth and focus.

The book has its own reversibility, of course, with regard to the Spanish and Portuguese languages. This fact should not discourage readers who only know one language or the other. I consider chapter 1 to be indispensable, but beyond that, each major chapter can be read in isolation. However, I am optimistic, because of the comprehensive interests of many scholars and because of the intimacy of the languages, which are like two sides of the same woven tablecloth, that there will be a number of readers who will want to read the entire book and will find no great difficulty in doing so.

This study involves the interplay of a number of opposing tendencies: theory versus practice, reader contribution versus textual contribution in interpretation, mimetic art versus nonmimetic art, and critical attitudes positing determinacy of meaning versus those positing indeterminacy. If I seem noncommital about some of these oppositions, I hope it will be seen as a commitment of another kind, to parsimony and pluralism.

REVERSIBLE READINGS

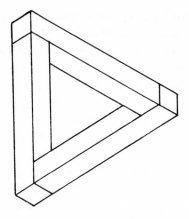

Fig. 1.1. The Penrose "impossible object"

1
Ambiguity in
Artistic Expression

The concept of ambiguity as it pertains to this book is vividly illustrated in certain depictions of "impossible objects," which at once seem to captivate and confuse the mind of the observer. For example, in the drawing by Penrose and Penrose[1] (fig. 1.1), conventional techniques of perspective strongly suggest to the mind a three-dimensional object. When the eye is led to the corners of the triangular structure, however, the idea of three dimensions is confounded. The impression of solid mass in the three sides is incompatible with the way those sides are connected, so upon observing the figure we are apt to oscillate between conflicting perceptions. Besides this ambiguity of two versus three dimensions, we find one of perspective. Is the figure seen from above, or from below? The ambiguity exemplified by this figure might be called an "ambiguity of impossibilities," because it leads to a particular conclusion (that the figure represents a three-dimensional object), and then makes that conclusion impossible.

The following figure (fig. 1.2) typifies ambiguity in its converse form, which may be called "ambiguity of possibilities." We may interpret this drawing by Winson[2] as a representation either of an Indian's head or of an Eskimo's entire body seen from the rear. Certain features of the sketch belong primarily to one interpretation or the other, such as the Eskimo's right hand, the Eskimo's feet, or the lines that create details on the Indian's brow and his ear. However, both interpretations are equally possible. Both are likewise mutually incompatible. In other words, we cannot see both things at once, for, when we perceive the drawing as an Indian the details that suggest an

Eskimo become incorporated into the Indian's features, and when we perceive it as an Eskimo, the Indian's features either become the Eskimo's, or sink into the background. This sketch may not have the disturbing effect of the previous one, because we can achieve a "stable" perception of one object or the other. Nevertheless, it may still cause an ambivalent sensation as the mind alternately perceives the two pictures.

These drawings have their counterparts in several other media. The medium of prose seems particularly akin to drawing in

Fig. 1.2.
Winson's Indian/Eskimo figure

its ability to *represent* objects—to create in the observer's mind the illusion of a solid reality. The force of the "ut pictura poesis" tradition provides strong justification for comparing literary art with representational painting or sketching. However, with both visual and verbal art, the illusion may be created *and* confounded. In this examination of four Latin American novels I will focus upon this confounding tendency. I will attempt to show that each of the novels contains the sort of equivocal information displayed in the visual figures, whereby we are presented with incompatible conclusions from a single source. Besides showing the structure of ambiguity in the works, I will try in the study to explain how such ambiguity contributes to the total artistic effect of each work.

Coexisting Mutually Exclusives

Because people use the word "ambiguity" in many ways, it is necessary to define as exactly as possible the way I intend to employ it in this study. As the visual examples suggest, the phenomenon to be examined and defined as ambiguity is more specific than that of any double meaning or indeterminate meaning. One well-formulated definition of ambiguity that applies precisely to this concept is by Shlomith Rimmon in her book, *The Concept of Ambiguity—the Example of James*.

Rimmon begins her explanation of ambiguity with a short introductory lesson in logic, because her formula is based on accepted logical operations. Logical operations work with internally verifiable sentences called propositions to construct "molecular" sentences out of "atomic" sentences. There are five propositional operations, which join the smaller sentences into larger sentences—one monary and four binary. These may be denoted with the following symbols:[3]

monary   1. negation: $\underline{a}$ (not a)
binary   2. conjunction, product: a.b (a and b)
        3. disjunction, sum: a$\lor$b (a or b)
        4. implication: a $\ni$ b (a implies b)
        5. equivalence: a = b (a is equivalent to b)

The operation of disjunction requires further explanation because it is at the heart of the formula for ambiguity. There are two types of disjunction—exclusive or strong and inclusive or weak. Inclusive disjunction means that *a* is true or *b* is true or both may be true. Rimmon's example is the sentence, "Customers who are teachers or college students are entitled to a special reduction." The intention is that customers who are both teachers and college students, as well as those who are one or the other, will be entitled to a special reduction. The exclusive disjunction means that a may be true or b may be true, but that both a and b may not be true. Rimmon's example here is a parent's response to a child agitating to go on a hike and to go to the theater in a single afternoon: "No, we are going on a hike or we are going to the theater." The speaker would have in mind an exclusive disjunction—either a hike or a trip to the theater, but definitely not both.[4]

It is with the exclusive disjunction, often shown by the sign $\wedge$, that we will be concerned when we are talking about ambiguity. For the disjunction to be true, or in other words logical or based upon accepted notions of reality, there must be a relationship of contradiction or contrariness between its propositions. If proposition a is true, then proposition b must be false, and vice versa. Having established this, we may now introduce Rimmon's definition of ambiguity. According to her, literary ambiguity is a "conjunction" of propositions in exclusive disjunction:

> Ambiguity, in the sense in which I propose to employ the term, can be defined with the help of the following ad hoc formula: a $\wedge$ b. The symbol " $\wedge$ " is not simply a logical connector, but a relational sign which combines an exclusive disjunction and a conjunction in the following way: The exclusive disjunction is taken in its strict logical sense, while the conjunction is given the sense of copresence in the literary text. The " $\wedge$ " sign implies that if the disjunction is true, the relation between a and b is such that if a is true b must be false and vice versa. . . . When the interdependence between a and b is such that if one is true the other must be false, the truth-value of a.b is "F" [false], while that of a$\wedge$b is "T," taking one of the following forms:

A	B	A∧B
T	F	T
F	T	T

But as soon as we are confronted with a specific ambiguous text and we wish to decide which member of the disjunction is true and which is false, a serious problem arises. On the one hand, we know that in an analogous life-situation we would have to choose between the two alternatives, logic instructing us that only one member of an exclusive disjunction is true and the other is false. On the other hand, there is in the case of ambiguity equal evidence for the truth and falsity of both a and b. We cannot decide whether a or b is the true proposition and, consequently, which of the two is the false one. Both possibilities thus remain equitenable and copresent. Although a conjunction in the logical sense would yield "F" as its truth-value, the narrative or verbal expressions as a whole are "true" and so are their constituent "propositions." Thus some kind of "conjunction" is established between the exclusive disjunction, and the incongruent "∧" marks precisely the tension we feel between the impulse to choose and the arrest of that impulse by the realization of the equitenability of mutual exclusives.[5]

A simple example of a pattern in fiction that may be described by the formula a ∧ b is Jorge Luis Borges' "El Sur" (1941).[6] This tale tells about the death of Juan Dahlmann, an Argentine bureaucrat with a romantic temperament. In accordance with clues from the text, one may reasonably formulate two conclusions, called by Rimmon "finalized hypotheses,"[7] about how he died.

The first conclusion, corresponding, let us say, to proposition a in the disjunction, is that Dahlmann is killed in a knife battle outside a store in the South of Argentina. This is according to the explicit narration, and assumes that Dahlmann actually took the train southward from Buenos Aires toward his "estancia" in order to recuperate after nearly dying from blood poisoning following an accident. The second conclusion, proposition *b*, is that Dahlmann remains in his hospital, that his southern voyage is a wish-fulfilling hallucination, product of a relapse, and that his death in a violent confrontation is his own mental compensation for a most unheroic death. Various points in the text emphasize the symmetry of Dahlmann's voyage with respect to events surrounding his entry into the hospital, and therefore suggest that the journey is but a transformation of other events.

The two propositions are in exclusive disjunction. That is to say, they cannot both be true. If Dahlmann dies in the Buenos Aires hospital, he cannot have died in the primitive South, and vice versa. However, textual evidence seems to give equal credence to both propositions. In this sense, then, there is a conjunction between the two propositions. As Rimmon says, "The incongruent ' /\ ' marks precisely the tension we feel between the impulse to choose and the arrest of that impulse by the realization of the equitenability of mutual exclusives."

Types of Exclusive Propositions

Having introduced the term "proposition" in our explanation of ambiguity, we should explain that, by definition, a proposition must be expressed in a sentence. Propositions in relation to artistic works are based on something they say or mean. In the case of "El Sur," the meanings comprising the mutually exclusive propositions are easy to perceive, for they are located in the story's plot: (1) Dahlmann's journey is real, versus (2) Dahlmann's journey is imaginary. Both propositions involve the object that is represented through the story's language— Juan Dahlmann's journey. In Winson's drawing, the dual propositions also involve what is represented—either Eskimo or Indian.

Very often, however, an ambiguity arises between the representational realm and a nonrepresentational realm. For example, the drawing by Penrose and Penrose seems to present the propositions: (1) the figure represents a material object, versus (2) the figure does not represent a material object. The referential character of words can also be subject to ambiguity, particularly in the case of poetry, where there often exists what Valéry has called "hesitation between the sound and the sense."[8] Sound (the nonreferential quality of words) competes with sense (the referential capacity of language) for control of the reader's or listener's perception.[9]

Ambiguity, then, may feature conflicting hypotheses of the following types: representational versus representational (as in "El Sur" and the Indian-Eskimo picture), and representational versus nonrepresentational (as in the Penrose drawing). In addition, it is possible for ambiguity to involve conflicting hypotheses, both or all of which are nonrepresentational. For example, in the sonnet there is a purely structural ambiguity. The quatrains and tercets each have two stanzas. Considering this, we have distinct pairs of stanzas that seem to balance each other as equals. However, because the quatrains have four lines and the tercets only three, they are at the same time unequal. We have "two equals two" on the one hand, versus "eight does not equal six" on the other. Music, which is by nature nonreferential, displays ambiguities of this type. Leonard Bernstein, for example, speaks of ambiguity in music between tonality and chromaticism, between competing rhythms and between different musical structures within the same sequence.[10]

The Ambiguity of "Ambiguity"

Rimmon's concept of ambiguity, while not entirely her own creation,[11] does not correspond precisely to the way many people have used the word. One reason for this lack of agreement about ambiguity is that, as if by poetic justice, the term "ambiguity" is itself ambiguous. Webster gives these two rather incompatible definitions for the word "ambiguous": (1) doubtful or uncertain, and (2) capable of being understood in two or more possible senses. The first of these definitions seems to imply that the ambiguous sign is somehow undercharged with meaning—that it is vague or unclear, while the second suggests a supercharging of the sign, so that it can have multiple meanings, each of which may be perfectly clear. This relates to the dual meaning of the prefix *ambi-*, which may signify *bothness* or being on both sides at once, as in "ambidextrous" and "ambivalent," or may also signify *aroundness,* as in the case of "ambient" or "ambit." While the first implies clearly distinguishable meanings, the second implies a kind of indirection or vagueness. Webster's second definition is more nearly like our working definition, but still much broader because the multiple meanings are not necessarily exclusive.

The problem of the term's imprecision made its way into William Empson's pioneering work, *Seven Types of Ambiguity* (1930). Empson used the word in a rather general sense, characterizing ambiguity in his first edition as "any consequence of language, however slight, which adds some nuance to the direct statement of prose." Such a definition makes room for any number of devices within the scope of ambiguity. Empson acknowledged in a revised edition that the definition "stretches the term 'ambiguity' so far that it becomes almost meaningless," and modified his definition to include "any verbal nuance, however slight, which gives room for alternative reactions to the same piece of language." Although closer to Rimmon's, this definition still gives room for the consideration of various types of multiple meaning. Furthermore, Empson did little to make his original text conform to his later definition, and admits in the later edition that "the question of

what would be the best definition of 'ambiguity' (whether the
example in hand should be called ambiguous) crops up all
through the book."[12]

If "ambiguity" is taken to refer to any instance where multiple reactions or meanings are obtainable from the same expression, it becomes a global sort of term, in which such divergent
phenomena as metaphor, allegory, irony, symbolism, and
vagueness may be included. However, ambiguity is not simply
the composite of other such types of multiple signification. A
definition specifying that multiple meanings be mutually exclusive makes "ambiguity" refer to communicative phenomena
that have not normally been called by another name.

In accordance with her specific definition, Rimmon has developed a set of criteria that the ambiguous expression must
meet. A review of these conditions will help illustrate the difference between ambiguity in the sense of mutually exclusive
propositions, and other phenomena often called ambiguous:

1. An ambiguous expression has two or more distinct meanings operating in the given context.

2. The meanings of an ambiguous expression are not reduci-
ble to each other, or to some common denominator, nor are they
identifiable with each other or subsumable in a larger unit of
meaning which they conjoin to create or in which they are
reconciled or integrated.

3. The meanings of an ambiguous expression are mutually
exclusive in the context, in the sense that if one applies, the
other cannot apply, and vice versa.

4. Hence, an ambiguous expression calls for choice between
its alternative meanings, but at the same time provides no
ground for making the choice. The mutually exclusive meanings therefore coexist in spite of the either/or conflict between
them.[13]

All of these criteria employ the word "meanings." For present purposes, we will consider meaning to be an idea or mes-

sage that may be transmitted from a sender to a receiver, by means of a set of data generated by the sender. We will assume that meaning does not reside within the signs of the data, nor is it projected upon the data by the receiver, but rather that it is product of a kind of transaction[14]—the result of a process by which the receiver gathers evidence from his set of data, formulates hypotheses based upon his data, and corrects or modifies his hypotheses upon coming into contact with new information. As this process continues, he is able to form increasingly more workable hypotheses until he reaches what Rimmon calls a "finalized hypothesis."[15] This finalized hypothesis is the "meaning" as Rimmon uses the term. Thus, ambiguity involves mutually exclusive hypotheses, generated by the observer based on data that is in some way multidirective.

A frequent heuristic device used by readers, which has the effect of focusing attention upon the text, is to speak of meaning as being "in" the text. At times this may hardly seem to be a figure of speech, but in the strict sense it has to be. Written messages, strictly speaking, do not contain meaning. Rimmon occasionally uses this device, such as in the definition quoted where she speaks of the copresence of mutually exclusive propositions in the literary text. In all likelihood, she is referring more exactly to data in the text that give cause for formulating mutually exclusive hypotheses.

We will posit that artistic works have the capacity for determinacy of meaning, that is, for meaning very much the same thing to any number of careful observers.[16] An author achieves this consensus much in the same way that a successful trial lawyer obtains his aim in court—by selection and logical presentation of evidence. Obviously consensus is often not the case in our reaction to artistic works. When disputable or disparate reactions occur with respect to some text, the lack of agreement may be caused by several factors.

Other Expressions, Polysemic but Unambiguous

Diverging reactions are a natural outcome when several people experience art. The fact that an array of different reactions occurs does not necessarily mean that those interpreting the work disagree with each other. Rather they may simply be looking at different nonexclusive aspects of the same work. Differences in critical focus should not be confused with conflicting conclusions, which are a feature of ambiguous expression.

Even when contradictory interpretations abound concerning a given work, there may be no authentic ambiguity as it has been defined here. One needs to determine to what extent such conflicting interpretations are supported by evidence from the text. Many conclusions may be more intuitive or impressionistic than textually founded. There will always be divergent subjective reactions to literature, but such disparities are not always evidence of ambiguity as they may be more a projection of the individual psyche of the reader than they are a product of the text.

Some forms of expression, whether by design or otherwise, are sufficiently amorphous as to give little or no direction as to how they should be interpreted. This appears to be the case with many modern works called "open works." Umberto Eco characterizes open works as works that lack "centers of orientation."[17] Although such works have often been called ambiguous, they are not really so according to the present definition, for ambiguity as defined in our study is the product of two or more well-defined centers of orientation, which happen to be in exclusive contradiction, rather than the product of the absence of centers of orientation. The multiple interpretations that may result from "open works" result from language's capability for nondeterminacy of meaning, whereas ambiguity results from language's capability for determinancy of meaning. Actually, an ambiguous work is a sort of "half-open" work. It is neither subject to an infinity of interpretations nor explainable by a single interpretation. Rather, there are a few exclusive readings.

Another type of work, often called ambiguous, is the work that emphasizes the role of the reader in experiencing art and encourages his participation by giving him choices in the reading of the work—choices regarding reading sequence, selection of passages, or other factors. Julio Cortázar's *Rayuela* (Argentina, 1963) is an example of such a work, as are *Blanco* and *Discos visuales* (Mexico, 1967, 1968) by Octavio Paz. These phenomena are actually quite dissimilar from ambiguity under our definition, because the only choice encouraged by ambiguity is a well-defined choice between two or more mutually exclusive propositions. These "open works" and "participatory works" do not attest to any unavoidable ambiguity in language, because it might be argued that consensus in meaning is not their goal. Continuing with the courtroom analogy, we may say that readers of an ambiguous work are like a hung jury, unable to decide between alternatives. Readers of open or participatory works, on the other hand, are not like a jury at all, because they are not required to choose among a limited set of "verdicts."

Occasionally, diverging opinions concerning a work are clues to an authentic ambiguity. Incomplete interpretations may exist because of careless reading, criticism that seeks to overclarify, or a certain abiding disdain for ambiguity[18] which regards it as undesirable in art the way it often is in diplomacy or business. For any or all of these reasons, opinions have generally come out on either side of the question before the synthesizing acknowledgment of ambiguity is made. For example, we will see that this is the case with Machado de Assis' novel *Dom Casmurro*, which has inspired and continues to inspire a polemic over whether the female protagonist, Capitu, is innocent or guilty of adultery charges. Polemics of this kind, where opinions are divided on both sides of an issue that cannot be resolved by careful definition of terms, tend to suggest in themselves the irreconcilability of mutually exclusive propositions that characterizes ambiguity.

In summary, not all works that generate disparate reactions can be considered to contain ambiguous expressions. Ambiguity by our definition is more a distinctive feature of certain types of expression than a trait common to all language.

Few of the rhetorical devices that involve multiplicity of meaning qualify as ambiguity in the sense we intend to use the term, although all have perhaps been called ambiguity at one time or another. Allegory, for example, is not ambiguity. Esteban Echeverría's "El matadero" (Argentina, written 1838) is an allegory wherein savage behavior in a slaughter yard is made equivalent to the barbarism of the Rosas regime (1829–52) in Argentina. In this case, the double meanings are parallel and mutually supporting. However, the situation of ambiguity requires that the two interpretations be in opposition rather than equivalence.

Metaphor is a similar device involving equivalent meanings, but not necessarily ambiguity. Some have seen in the tenement house of Aluísio Azevedo's *O cortiço* (Brazil, 1890) the metaphor of a human or animal body. In this example, the reader is at no point required to choose between the dual meanings. The device of ambiguity, however, would require a choice.

Often one message seems to be subsumable in a broader, more inclusive message. The aimless, angry battles of the revolutionaries in Mariano Azuela's *Los de abajo* (Mexico, 1915) may be interpreted in existentialist terms as the individual's anxious search for meaning. If such is the case, there is no ambiguity, for the more immediate meaning expands to fit the more universal one, and is not at odds with it.

The common practice of employing a concrete image to represent an abstraction, often called symbolism, is likewise not ambiguity. In Graciliano Ramos' *Vidas secas* (Brazil, 1938), a bed with leather strappings seems to symbolize Vitória's hopes. Both the bed and the concept of Vitória's hopes may coexist. Because the reader does not need to decide between the concrete image and the abstraction it suggests, the exclusivity that characterizes ambiguity is not present.

The case of irony is more similar to ambiguity than some devices, for in irony according to the traditional rhetorical definition there is in fact a disjunction between two propositions— one that is expressed and another that is implied or intended. However, with irony the propositions are not equitable; by definition, one invalidates the other. José Cândido de Carvalho's *O coronel e o lobisomem* (Brazil, 1964) exemplifies this concept of irony. The bombastic narrator, Coronel Ponciano Azeredo Furtado, portrays himself as a heroic figure. However, behind his back an "implied narrator" gives another version of the colonel as a vulnerable, overgrown child. The reader is not forced to make an impossible choice between the two characterizations. On the contrary, it is made clear that the childlike characterization is the valid one. If the choice were not so clear, the device might be considered ambiguous. But then, by definition, it would cease to be ironic because the successful instance of irony involves the validity of what is implied over what is actually said.

Antithesis, paradox, and other polarized expressions are occasionally designated by the term ambiguity. Normally, however, they are not ambiguous because no choice between the two poles is really necessary. Machado de Assis offers an example of paradox in his characterization of Simão Bacamarte, protagonist in "O alienista" (1882): "Simão Bacamarte achou em si os característicos de perfeito equilíbrio mental e moral; pareceu-lhe que possuía a sagacidade, a paciência, a perseverança, a tolerância, a veracidade, o vigor moral, a lealdade, todas as

qualidades enfim que podem formar um acabado mentecapto."[19] The statement's seemingly contradictory description of Bacamarte as being both "um acabado mentecapto" and
a man with "perfeito equilíbrio mental e moral" can easily be
resolved by defining terms. Insanity, by Bacamarte's revised
definition, consists of being abnormal. The observable norm in
the depicted society is mental and moral disequilibrium; therefore, the stable ones in the society are crazy. Because there is
no real disjunction involved in the statement, but only an apparent one, ambiguity does not really exist. On the other hand,
other expressions called paradoxes do not resolve themselves,
and seem to qualify as ambiguous statements. The "liar paradox" ("don't believe me because I'm lying") is an example. The
proposition that the speaker should be believed excludes the
equally plausible proposition that the speaker should not be
believed. In fact, belief requires disbelief and vice versa. This
sort of paradox, employing mutual exclusives in compact self-
cancellation, is analogous to the Penrose drawing with its disturbing fluctuation of impressions.

Antithesis is a prominent feature in Carlos Fuentes' characterization of Artemio in *La muerte de Artemio Cruz* (Mexico,
1962). The protagonist is alternately depicted as cowardly, au-
dacious, loving, hateful, patriotic, and traitorous. These strong
contrasts in his depiction do not involve ambiguity, however,
because no choice is required between the conflicting values.
The point is that Artemio is a combination of all those properties. Such an antithetical characterization creates complex
characters and works, but not necessarily ambiguity.

Finally, vague expressions have often been called ambiguous, but are not properly so according to our definition. Signs
are said to be vague when it is unclear within a given context to
what the signs refer. As long as the context remains limited and
the signs are not further defined, their meaning remains
blurred and subject to guesswork by the interpreter. "Las

babas del diablo" (1959) by Julio Cortázar presents an example
of vague signs. A man with a camera comes across an encounter
between a woman and an adolescent boy. The boy seems ap-
prehensive. The photographer takes a picture of the pair, and is
discovered as he does so. The boy runs away while the woman is
joined by a man, and both berate the photographer. Any
number of interpretations can be drawn from the data provided
(the description provided here may have already added some
subjective interpretation). The story examines some of the possibilities, and emphasizes the subjective and equivocal nature
of the conclusions. In the story the photograph suggests concretely the phenomenon of signs in a limited temporal and
spatial context. The important motif of the projected enlarge-
ment or "blowup" suggests the mind's reaction to vague data—
a projection of subjective judgments upon it, which may
change with each new contemplation. While vague expressions
encourage subjective interpretations and are likely to prompt
such questions in the interpreter's mind as who, what, where,
why, or how, ambiguous expressions, by our definition, supply
enough data to oblige the observer to choose between more or
less determinate hypotheses. The question prompted by ambiguity is *which*?

Even though vagueness and ambiguity are different communicative phenomena, the two are often closely related in practice. Vague signs, which in themselves are not ambiguous, may
become ambiguous when placed in the proper context. In the
sentence, "Joan's friend waved to her father," two propositions
seem to be possible: that Joan's friend waved to her own father,
or that she waved to Joan's father. An ambiguous statement
centers around the vagueness of the possessive pronoun "her."
"Her" by itself does not suggest mutually exclusive propositions. Rather, the word acts as a kind of fulcrum upon which
words like "Joan's" and "friend" act to create alternative meanings. Thus, vagueness is very often a contributing component

to ambiguity. To return to the dual etymologic meaning of *ambi-* mentioned earlier, it might be said that while our definition of ambiguity definitely involves the "bothness" of mutually exclusive propositions, each given credence by the data presented, it might also often involve "aroundness." Component signs within the overall ambiguous structure may be indeterminate enough to provide pivotal points upon which the more rigid signs are able to swing in their interplay between established alternatives. In a discussion of Mallarmé, Jacques Derrida points out the poet's use of images such as creases, folds, and birds' wings to symbolize the disjunctive capacity of language.[20] In each of these images, there are two planes or plane-

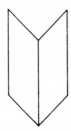

Fig. 1.3. An ambiguous folded paper

like structures that revolve upon a central axis. One of the classic examples of visually ambiguous figures constitutes this very image as seen in figure 1.3. In this representation of a folded paper, do the halves point towards us or away from us? As we weigh these alternatives, the paper seems practically to flap back and forth like a pair of wings, upon the uncertain axis of the central crease. The "bothness" of the paper surface interacts with the "aroundness" of the crease to create the ambiguous figure. In the same manner, language, rigidly clear, pointing in contradictory directions, seems often to interact with pivotal vagueness to create ambiguity in verbal expression.

To some degree, all representational art is vague. The piece of art is a finite, self-sufficient artifact. Details that would be available in reality are missing in the representation. Our imaginations quite naturally supply these missing details, so we achieve an impression of a "presence." Ambiguous art often exploits this vagueness, and represents two or more conflicting realities, which our imaginative sense of coherence may be at a loss to account for.

Ambiguity's Effects on the Reader

Although the most appropriate time to discuss the artistic effects of ambiguity is in the analysis of the novels, where I can provide specific examples, I will offer a few general observations here as a preview. As he discovers his inability to resolve the conflicting hypotheses, the reader is initially apt to react in one of two ways. A reasonable first reaction is to reexamine the information presented by the work. This seems to be one of the primary artistic functions of ambiguity—drawing the observer into a more intimate confrontation with the work of art. The observer's problem-solving instinct is alternately excited and frustrated, and until he is convinced that the problem is impossible he searches the work's patterns and signs more and more carefully. In this manner ambiguity brings about a "de-automatization"[21] in the observer's response to language, which has been called the principal function of artistic communication.

Once the possibility of resolving the ambiguity through search has been exhausted, the reader might well give up the quest. This renunciation of the worldly problem-solving mentality in relation to a work of art seems to be a significant esthetic matter, for it calls for recognition of the work of art as a work of art, recognition of the illusion, artifice, and imitation that are essential to so much of our artistic creation. As I intend to show later, this esthetic distancing can be both the final reaction as the observer comes to terms with the insoluble illusion of ambiguity, as well as one pole of an oscillating movement between disbelief and suspension of disbelief, which carries the observer through the process of reading or otherwise experiencing art.

So far we have discussed ambiguity as a situation where meanings are at war with each other. An idea I will explore in my examination of the individual works is that once we have recognized the impossibility of winning that war, we may be able to adopt a more distant perspective and consider the ambiguity of the work as a structure in itself, or as a single unit of meaning that may relate to other motifs or themes within the overall work. For instance, the irresolvable ambiguity between two different interpretations of a woman's attitude toward a man might be in itself a metaphor for the position of man in relation to existence, or of the reader in relation to his text. The disjunction of meanings, repeated in numerous variations, may be considered a theme in itself, and provide a thematic unity to the work.

Yet another function of artistic ambiguity is a psychological, perhaps, even spiritual function of transcending the mundane realm by creating or beholding the impossible. In the drawings accompanying this chapter we have seen that it is *possible* to create the impression of a concrete, three-dimensional object by placing lines on a two-dimensional page. Our minds are accustomed to seeing such lines arranged on a flat surface and making a concession or adjustment that allows us to see real objects as if they were present. Such is the *possibility* of representational figures. Language, with its interplay between sign and referent, has this same possibility. Its referential capacity is such that a few vivid words can make us imagine things as if they were part of our external world. Returning to the drawings, we observe that the techniques of representation can be manipulated so as to represent *impossible* objects—the three-dimensional figure that could not be three-dimensional or the

drawing that depicts two objects at once. The *impossibility* of
these objects, paradoxically, is only apprehended when we first
concede the possibility of their representation. Unless we acknowledge the capacity of lines to signify three-dimensional
objects, we see not an impossible object but simply a series of
connected lines. Ambiguity in language seems to operate upon
the same principle. We must accept the referential nature of
words before that referred-to reality can seem impossible in its
ambiguity. Artistic ambiguity, as we shall see, seems to involve
a plunge into the worldly in order to surmount the worldly. We
proceed for a while on this referential level, where all seems
clear and logical. But suddenly that realm becomes impossible.
That real-world impossibility is one of art's great possibilities, as
Rimmon explains:

> In life we cannot allow equal tenability to contradictories and
> although we sometimes realize that the information we have is
> insufficient for choice, choice itself always seems imperative.
> Art, on the other hand, makes the coexistence of contradicto-
> ries possible. . . . the triumph of art, rather than its bank-
> ruptcy, is celebrated by . . . ambiguity, showing not simply
> how the possible is rendered impossible by art, but mainly how
> the impossible becomes possible in it. [22]

Persons who look beyond the world have often been inclined
towards the contemplation or creation of objects uncharac-
teristic of natural life. [23] Artistic ambiguity as I have explained it
in this chapter may perhaps belong to this category of objects.
Expressed in lifelike terms, it encourages the illusion of a mundane reality that must be subjected to the test of logical truth.
That test tells us a choice between alternatives is imperative. In
the confounding of that choice, however, ambiguity gives us a
sense of another possibility beyond the concrete and the logical, and perhaps even a momentary feeling of transcendence
from an illusory, untrue world to a realm of richer truth.

2
Dom Casmurro as Undertow

The systematic and recursive nature of things is often reflected in a concentric analogy, where smaller structures mirror their more complex, containing structures, and vice versa. We look at the cell, and we can distinguish a microcosm of an organism, with the same essential functions of reproduction, nutrition, waste removal, and so on. We draw a diagram of an atom, and it reminds us of a solar system. In a limited sense, the same relation exists with narrative and its components: the story as a whole functions the same as a single sentence.

If the sentence is a microcosm of the overall narrative, we should not be surprised to find parallels between theories for analyzing narrative and those for analyzing sentences. In fact, much of the importance of linguistic theory for current theory of narrative is probably based on a comparison between sentence and story.[1] Titles of some important works on narrative, such as Todorov's *Grammaire du* Décaméron, Propp's *Morphology of the Folktale,* and Dorfman's *The Narreme in the Medieval Romance Epic* reflect this comparison. Central to these parallels is the concept of a dual structure in language in general and, more specifically, in narrative—some sort of deep, abstract or universal structure, in contrast to a structure that is at the surface, concrete and individualized.

One well-known linguistic theory based on this duality is that of Noam Chomsky. According to Chomsky's model an underlying grammar operates according to rules common to all languages, and produces structures with the basic components necessary for meaning, but not the peculiarities of specific languages. This is the *deep structure* of a language—its abstract, rudimentary form, perhaps similar to the thumbnail sketch of an architect, determining the essential structure, but not the actual details. On a higher level, a set of language-specific rules called *grammatical transformations* acts upon the deep structure to generate a structure that reflects the actual discourse of a particular language. The transformations yield a *surface structure,* which we might compare to a detailed blueprint—a relatively close representation of an expression as it might actually be realized. Examples of transformational rules are negation, deletion, specification of verb number, and use of the passive voice. According to Chomsky, these transformations account for the variety and creativity of language.[2]

Narrative also has its deep and surface structures. For example, the sequence: man and woman meet, they fall in love, the realization of their love is threatened, the obstacle is overcome, and they are united, is probably one of the most common deep structures in the universal grammar of narrative. The depth and universality of the structure is perhaps suggested by its legal status. It is in the public domain; that is, no one would think of calling anyone a plagiarist simply because his work derives from this common structure. Supplying the characters' names, creating specific circumstances, determining what moments of the drama are to be portrayed and what moments are to be left to the imagination, as well as many other artistic transformations, convert the deep structure into a surface structure. The term plagiarism might be applicable to the appropriation of these surface structures, but never to the use of deep structures.

Many theorists have attempted to identify deep structures and surface structures in narrative. The Russian formalists' *fabula* and *sužet* (often translated as *story* and *plot*), the structuralists' *histoire* and *discours* (influenced by another linguist's theoretical duality, Saussure's *langue* and *parole*), and the myth critics' *archetype* and *signature*[3] all identify a type of deep narrative structure (the first term in each case) and a type of surface structure. The deep structure is the story of a given work, stripped of all digressions, additions, or nonessential material until it cannot be further reduced without losing its causality. The individual events of the story have both a chronological and a causal ordering, although one or the other may predominate in one definition or another. The surface structure bears the mark of the individual teller, and may show reordering of the story's events, narration by implication through deletion of material, ornamental language, repetition, digression, selection of point of view, or any number of other devices. What is often not clear in the employment of the various terms roughly synonymous with surface structure is whether the terms refer to a structure within a specific medium—a book, a film, a play, etc., or a structure in more or less finalized artistic form, prior to its expression in a particular medium.[4] In reality, there seems to be in narrative art a pre-medium surface structure as well as a medium-bound "super surface structure." This is evidenced by the fact that a novel can often be converted into a film or vice versa, with rather close fidelity to an artistic surface structure although in an entirely different medium.

The distance or difference between a narrative's deep structure and surface structure may vary somewhat. In folktales or simple children's tales where the actions themselves tend to be more important than the reporting thereof, the transformations involved may be minimal and the distance between structures small. In more literary, artistic narratives, the distance is necessarily greater, for the artistic quality is in the transformations themselves; the more craft in the work, the more significant the transformations involved and the greater distance between the narrative's deep and surface structures.

Machado de Assis' *Dom Casmurro* is a good example of a narrative with a great distance between its deep structure and its surface structure. A study of the stylistic devices apparent in the novel is essentially a study of the artistic transformations involved in the production of a literary surface structure. A detailed examination of these devices is unnecessary here, both because considerable attention has already been dedicated to these matters[5] and because style itself is not my intended focus. The point I wish to make is that because of these stylistic transformations a considerable space is created between the work's surface and its underlying narrative sequence. We can tell someone in a moment what the novel's story is, but after doing so we are apt to feel dissatisfied for not having communicated what the work is really about. So much of what it is about is in the way it is expressed.

Interestingly, the novel hints at the notion of a transformed surface expression arising out of an underlying standard. For example, in the chapter "Uma reforma dramática" (chap. lxxii), the narrator proposes a reordering of stories in dramatic productions, so that "as peças começassem pelo fim."[6] A play could not "start at the end" if there were not some universal, underlying sense telling us what the end is. About two-thirds of the way into the novel, the narrator reaches the point of his departure from the seminary, and declares, "Aqui devia ser o meio do livro, mas . . . chego quase ao fim do papel" (chap. xcvii, p. 828), suggesting the artist's transformation in his particular expression of a preexisting abstract story structure.

Ambiguity and Underlying Structures

Having suggested that a novel contains both a surface structure and an underlying structure, we may use these concepts to examine the ambiguity in *Dom Casmurro*. In a discussion of ambiguity on the level of the sentence, Chomsky refers to ambiguous sentences as those that can have two or more nonequivalent deep structures. One of his examples is the sentence, "I know a taller man than Bill," which might have deep structures rendered verbally as "I know a taller man than Bill does," and "I know a taller man than Bill is."[7]

Narrative ambiguity may be similarly defined. Let us now return to the concept of narrative deep structure and surface structure. We defined the deep structure of a particular narrative as its story, reduced to its essential actions, in causal and temporal order. The surface structure is the narrative's concrete expression. We may define narrative ambiguity, then, as the existence of more than one deep structure (essential story line) underlying a single surface structure (text). This definition brings us face to face with Shlomith Rimmon's concept of ambiguity, discussed in chapter 1 as the copresence of mutually exclusive propositions in a given text. A deep structure is in essence an abstract underlying proposition.[8] Perhaps the only significant distinction between Rimmon's concept and our linguistic analogy is that for Rimmon the contradictory meanings are *in* the surface structure—"we can discern two mutually exclusive *fabulas* in the same *sužet*,"[9] while Chomsky would probably say that the contradictory meanings are *underlying* the surface expression. Although both may be workable definitions, the latter seems preferable, because to say a proposition is "in" a text is like saying a meaning is "in" a word. Although for practical purposes it might be acceptable to say so, it is a failure to distinguish between sign and referent.

While Chomsky does not emphasize the mutually exclusive aspect of the underlying structures, his qualifier "non-equivalent" means essentially the same thing on the level where he is working. Two nonequivalent deep structures of a given sentence are bound to be mutually exclusive. By the same token, it is hard to conceive of two nonequivalent narrative deep structures that would not be mutually exclusive when reduced to their most abstract, nonindividualized state. Going back to the sentence "I know a taller man than Bill," we see that the underlying notions "than Bill is" and "than Bill knows" are mutually exclusive in the sense that the sentence can communicate one notion or the other, but not both at once.

A distinguishing feature of *Dom Casmurro* is the existence of two possible underlying narrative structures, or in other words, two mutually exclusive readings. The pivotal concern of the narrative is Capitu's fidelity or infidelity to her husband, Bentinho. On the one hand, evidence within the text encourages us to conclude that she committed adultery with her husband's best friend, while on the other hand it seems to support the conclusion that she was the falsely accused victim of her husband's overactive imagination.

Critics and the Novel's Ambiguity

The question of Capitu's guilt or innocence has been irresistible to the critics. Keith Ellis' review of significant criticism on the matter, now somewhat dated, says that for a generation the critical approach was based on the assumption of her guilt, showing total acceptance of Bentinho's point of view as narrator.[10] Ellis' 1965 article was one of the first studies[11] to bring out the unresolvability of the puzzle: "It would seem that, in *Dom Casmurro*, Machado has discredited the effectiveness of either the provable guilt or provable innocence of Capitu, and has indelibly branded this aspect of the novel with the mark of ambiguity."[12] Since then, many others have acknowledged that ambiguity.[13]

Despite these acknowledgments, the tendency to take sides has remained. Interestingly, several critics lately have agreed that the novel presents an enigma, but then have proceeded to solve it rather than examine the tenability of both sides.[14]

If early one-sided interpretations of the novel were based on acceptance of the narrator's point of view, then later ones have tended to be based upon extratextual evidence. Helen Cald-

well's case for Capitu's innocence is founded largely on similarities seen between *Dom Casmurro* and *Othello*. Eugênio
Gomes relies on parallels with Zola's novel, *Madeleine Férat*
(1868). Wilson Martins' case against Bentinho's wife is based on
the thesis that "Guiomar [protagonist in Machado's *A mão e a
luva* (1874)] was actually a first draft of Capitu and that *The
Hand and the Glove* was a preliminary version of the more
successful *Dom Casmurro*."[15] Such attempts at concluding one
way or the other can be no more reliable than the earlier alliances with the narrator, for they fail to take into account that
no matter how striking a parallel between two texts may seem,
it thrives on differences as well as similarities. In all cases
where *Dom Casmurro* parallels another work, Capitu's action
could be either a point of comparison or a point of contrast.
Perhaps more than anything, this hearkening to similar texts
shows the difficulty of presenting a clear case for or against
Capitu using intrinsic evidence. An examination of this intrinsic evidence leads to the conclusion shared by relatively few
pieces of criticism—that the enigma must remain unsolved.
Once this relatively passive acknowledgment of ambiguity has
been made, the way remains open for an active analysis of the
system of clues that creates the work's epistemological impasse.

A Mechanism of Ambiguity

One of the grammatical transformations functioning in the
derivation of surface sentences from their underlying structures is that of deletion. The sentence, "I know a taller man
than Bill," discussed previously, exemplifies the deletion transformation, where what is deleted from the deep structure is an
abstraction corresponding to either "is" or "does." Any narrative is sure to have similar deletions in its surface structure,
because it is impractical if not impossible to depict through
language every detail perceived in a particular experience.

Because the reader readily fills in gaps created by such deletions using his imagination—a process called elucidation by
Monroe Beardsley[16]—nothing is necessarily lost because of
these deletions. The lacunae are not only a practical necessity,
but often an artistic one as well. Machado displayed an
awareness of the artistic desirability of withholding certain details, in his criticism of Eça de Queirós' novel, *O primo Basílio*
(Portugal, 1878).[17] According to his comments, not only is the
deletion of details a matter of taste, especially where such
themes as adultery are concerned, but it is also a purely artistic
matter. Too many details interfere with the clarity of images in
the reader's mind. In *Dom Casmurro*, Bento makes a similar
observation:

> . . . tudo se pode meter nos livros omissos. Eu quando leio
> algum desta outra casta, não me aflijo nunca. O que faço, em
> chegando ao fim, é cerrar os olhos e evocar todas as cousas que
> não achei nele. Quantas idéias finas me acodem então! Que de
> reflexões profundas! Os rios, as montanhas, as igrejas que não vi
> nas folhas lidas, todos me aparecem agora com as suas águas, as
> suas árvores, os seus altares, e os generais sacam das espadas
> que tinham ficado na bainha, e os clarins soltam as notas que
> dormiam no metal, e tudo marcha com uma alma imprevista.
> (Chap. lix, p. 792)

Dom Casmurro is a "livro omisso" par excellence, for the
artistic transformation of deletion has great importance in the
work. As we saw in Chomsky's sentence about knowing a taller
man than Bill, deletion can create ambiguity.[18] This is surely
the case in *Dom Casmurro*. The pivotal point of the novel's
ambiguity is a sexual relationship, which is not itself expressed
in the surface narrative. The narrator calls our attention to this
deletion in an ingenious way. The closest he ever comes to
providing an image of the sexual act at the center of the matter
is to evoke a set of sheets. Alluding to the evidence against

Desdemona in *Othello* and commenting on current trends for using more explicit details, he says: "Os lenços perderam-se, hoje são precisos os próprios lençóis; alguma vez nem lençóis há, e valem só as camisas" (chap. cxxxv; p. 859). What *Dom Casmurro*'s surface structure does, in essence, is provide us with a pair of sheets. What goes on between them is essential to grasping the deep structure of the work. But it is also a matter of making inferences based on other clues of the surface text. Because these details are further removed from the act than a pair of sheets ("alguma vez nem lençóis há") and because they can often be interpreted in mutually exclusive ways, we have the possibility of arriving at two incompatible readings of the novel.

Rimmon has developed tools for analyzing ambiguity's system of clues. By her formula, there is a type of syntax operating between motifs (clues) that allows for ambiguity to be produced in several ways.[19] Clue a supporting proposition a may be countered by a clue supporting contrary proposition b. We may refer to the clue supporting proposition a by writing $a+$, and to the clue supporting proposition b by writing $b+$. Clue $a+$ or $b+$ may be cancelled by a contradictory clue or, in other words, one that simply negates proposition a or b,[20] as in the combinations $a+$, $a-$ or $b+$, $b-$. Or, because of the contextual situation, a single clue may actually be doubly directed—a/b. Numerous permutations of these clue combinations are possible. In all cases, we can say we have an ambiguous narrative if there is an approximate equilibrium between contrary or contradictory clues—$a+b+a+b+$; $a+a-a+a-$; $a+b+a-b-$; a/b a/b a/b; etc.

Dom Casmurro involves a combination of these patterns of mutually exclusives. The story hinges upon two main propositions, which can be stated as follows:

1. Capitu is unfaithful to Bentinho $(a+)$.
2. Capitu is faithful to Bentinho $(a-)$.

These propositions are the center of mutually exclusive stories underlying the surface expression of the novel. While the
propositions are contradictory, that is, one is the negation of the
other, the deep structures into which they are incorporated are
not simply negatives of each other. Each story in the deep
structure contains not only one of the central propositions mentioned, but also a set of causes and effects associated with the
respective proposition. While it is possible for propositions to
be contradictories $(a+a-)$, it seems impossible for two essential stories, or narrative deep structures, to be contradictories.
One cannot tell a story, $a-$, in terms of what is not done (John
did not see Ann, they did not fall in love, etc.). For this reason,
we must speak of the exclusive deep structures underlying
Dom Casmurro as contrary deep structures $a+$ and $b+$.

Deep structure $a+$ conforms to the interpretation of Bento
Santiago, the narrator Dom Casmurro. Its essential elements
might be expressed thusly: Capitu, a young girl of a lower class,
desires to move upward. She uses her natural attractiveness to
encourage Bentinho, the rich boy next door, to fall in love with
her, which he does. Bentinho is forced to attend a seminary,
because his mother, Dona Glória, promised God to make her
son a priest. By sponsoring a substitute for Bentinho in the
priesthood, D. Glória fulfills her promise. Bentinho leaves the
seminary. Bentinho and Capitu are married. They want a child,
but cannot have one. After some time, Capitu has a son by
Escobar, Bentinho's friend from the seminary. The child Ezequiel's resemblance to Escobar causes Bentinho to remember
other incriminating evidence against Capitu and Escobar. Escobar drowns. When Capitu cries at his wake, Bentinho is
convinced of her guilt. He accuses Capitu, and gets a nonverbal
confession. The two are separated for life.

Deep structure $b+$ is the product of an extended play of
irony. Behind Santiago's back, as it were, an "implied narrator"
shows the unreliability of the first-person narrator's argument,

and presents another interpretation of the surface details: next-door neighbors Bentinho and Capitu fall in love. Bentinho is forced to attend a seminary, because his mother, D. Glória, promised God to make her son a priest. By sponsoring a sub-stitute for Bentinho in the priesthood, D. Glória fulfills her promise. Bentinho and Capitu are married. They want a child. After some time they have a son. A combination of circum-stances, physical resemblance, Bentinho's doubts about his own virility, and Capitu's natural attractiveness, makes Ben-tinho suspect that his friend from the seminary, Escobar, is the father of the child. Escobar drowns. When Capitu cries at his wake, Bentinho is convinced of her guilt. He accuses Capitu, who realizes the futility of trying to defend herself and refuses to do so. The two are separated for life.

We notice that about half the sentences in the first story summary are also found in the second. This is a characteristic pattern of ambiguous narratives—a combination of elements shared and not shared by deep structures which perhaps re-minds us of the shared and unshared lines in the Eskimo-Indian picture of chapter 1.

A System of Clues

Let us assume for the moment that the narrator's word can be relied upon. This is of course a very sizeable assumption. But it is an assumption that lies at the beginning of the reader's expe-rience of fiction. The reader seems by some tacit agreement to accept the narrator's information as true, and to ground his perception of the work's self-contained system on that basis, until he is instructed by the work itself to do otherwise. The revelation of the narrator's unreliability deserves our attention, particularly in the case of Machado's novel. But for now we will simply suspend that consideration, in the same manner that the reader begins by accepting Santiago's axiomatically reliable account. As was mentioned, the unequivocal facts of Capitu's fidelity or infidelity are missing from the account. Because we are not privy to what goes between the novel's "lençóis," we must make inferences, based upon its "lençóis," its "lenços," its "camisas," and whatever else we can lay hold of. Bentinho's belief that he was betrayed is the product of this same process of gathering evidence, followed by making inferences. Years later, Bento—we eliminate the diminutive ending to distinguish him from his younger self—will carefully present the evidence upon which Bentinho based his decision. That is not all Bento presents, however. He also gives plenty of clues incompatible with Bentinho's inferences.

It seems that Bentinho's conclusion that he has been betrayed rests on at least six underlying conclusions: (1) that Ezequiel is Escobar's son and not his own; (2) that Escobar has met with Capitu secretly; (3) that Capitu "confessed" involuntarily; (4) that Capitu loves Escobar; (5) that Capitu does not love Bentinho; and (6) that Capitu and Escobar are dishonest and conniving. These conclusions are arranged in approximate order of their relevance to the question of adultery, from most substantial to most circumstantial. We now take a look at the clues supporting or disclaiming each conclusion.

The conclusion that Ezequiel is Escobar's son and not Bentinho's is primarily based on two underlying conclusions. The first of these is that Ezequiel looks like Escobar. The similarity is acknowledged not only by Bentinho (chap. cxvi, pp. 857–58; chap. cxlv, p. 867) but also by Capitu herself (chap. cxxxi, p. 856; chap. cxxxviii, p. 862). The significance of the similarity is what is equivocal. As time goes on, the explanation of genetic inheritance emerges strongly in Bentinho's mind. There is the suggestion that even D. Glória sees the phenomenon that way—hence her acting "fria" (chap. cxv, p. 844) with Capitu.[21] D. Glória's live-in companion and cousin, Justina, suspects the same (chap. cxlv, p. 868). The interpretation of Ezequiel's physical similarity to Escobar as an inherited characteristic supports Bentinho's accusation of Capitu (a+). However, this reading is made ambiguous by the fact that Ezequiel "gosta de imitar os outros" (chap. cxii, p. 841). Because Bentinho's family has an intimate, friendly relationship with Escobar's, Ezequiel is perhaps more likely to imitate Escobar than anyone else (b+). Still another matter makes the genetic reading suspect— the physical similarity brought out much earlier between Capitu and the mother of her friend, Sancha, a similarity that can only be attributed to the fact that "na vida há dessas semelhanças esquisitas" (chap. lxxxiii, p. 815).

The second conclusion supporting the fatherhood of Escobar is that Bentinho may be sterile and incapable of producing a child. The only objective support for such a conclusion is the fact that both Bentinho and Capitu wanted a child, but could not have one for at least two years (chap. civ, pp. 833–34), and that Ezequiel was an only child. If Bentinho is sterile (b−), then Capitu must have gone elsewhere to conceive her much-desired child. A likely candidate is of course Escobar, whose fertility has been established by the fact that Sancha has borne him a daughter (we have no reason to suspect he is not the father). We must admit that this sort of evidence is hardly conclusive. Nevertheless, it is likely to seem important to someone like Bentinho, who is so insecure about his masculinity as to admit that Capitu "era mais mulher do que eu era homem" (chap. xxxi, p. 761).

The conclusion that Escobar and Capitu have secret meetings (a+) is most clearly suggested in the chapter "Embargos de terceiro." Instead of taking his wife to the opera as is his custom, Bentinho goes alone one night. Capitu "não foi por ter adoecido, mas quis por força que [Bentinho] fosse" (chap. cxii, p. 842). Bentinho returns home after the first act to find Escobar in the hall outside his door. The combination of Capitu's

insisting that Bentinho go without her, plus Escobar's unex-
pected presence at the house (clues supporting hypothesis $a+$)
are checked, however, by subsequent clues. One is Escobar's
explanation $(b+)$ that he has to consult Bentinho about an
urgent business matter: "Ocorrera um incidente importante,
e, tendo ele jantado na cidade, não quis ir para casa sem dizer-
me o que era" (chap. cxiii, p. 843). Furthermore, if the secret-
meeting hypothesis is correct, one would expect Capitu to hold
by her story of feeling sick. Instead, she claims she feels better,
and Escobar agrees that she looks well. These indications $(a-)$
go against the incriminating hypothesis, unless they are the
product of a kind of double dissimulation. If Capitu knows her
husband suspects her of feigning, she can undo or at least
hopelessly muddle that suspicion by behaving in the opposite
manner. She shows this sort of complex anticipatory thinking in
chapter lxxvi, when she demonstrates there is nothing between
her and a particular dandy passing by on horseback by acknowl-
edging she knows him and saying that such acknowledgment
"era prova exatamente de não haver nada entre ambos; se
houvesse era natural dissimular" (chap. lxxvi, p. 808). This dimension opens up the possibility in nearly all circumstances
that Capitu's seemingly transparent revelations are actually calculated to throw off suspicion.

Capitu acknowledges upon another occasion that Escobar
has been to the house in Bentinho's absence—to exchange
monetary notes Capitu has saved for ten pounds sterling (chap.
cvi, p. 835). Is this admission of a slightly indiscreet meeting a
disclosure of everything, or a revelation that actually hides
more than it discloses by disarming Bentinho's suspicion of
Capitu's feigning? We cannot tell; this and other disclosures are
doubly directed (a/b).

Bentinho believes that Capitu made involuntary confessions
of her guilt. In particular, he believes her glance at Escobar's
portrait, after he accuses her and Ezequiel runs into the room,

to be a confession (chap. cxxxix, p. 863). This matter in itself is
more like a space to be filled in by the observer than an actual
bit of evidence. It may in fact be a confession of guilt (a +), but it
may just as well be merely an acknowledgment of an arbitrary
"semelhança esquisita," or the beginning of an attempt to deny
any physical resemblance by comparing Ezequiel with the
photograph (a −). Another such incident is her chastisement of
José Dias for addressing her son as "filho do homem" (chap.
cxvi, p. 845). On the one hand, her agitation might indicate
that reference to the boy's paternity makes her nervous (a +).
On the other there are at least two possible nonincriminating
explanations (b +). First, she may find the address sacrilegious,
because the term is used in the Bible to refer to Christ, or
second, she may object to being left out of the picture; "filho do
homem" ignores the mother's part in bearing and rearing the
boy. On other occasions Capitu, unknowingly or not, makes
statements capable of exciting suspicion. For example, she
points out mannerisms in Ezequiel not typical of either her or
Bentinho: "Não sai a nós" (chap. cxii, p. 841). Later, she even
notes the similarity between Ezequiel's eyes and Escobar's
(chap. cxxxi, p. 856). Are these revelations unthinking, innocent small talk or calculated revelations aimed at deflating Bentinho's suspicion of her dissimulation? Doubly directive as they
are, the clues could just as easily be either.

Actually the whole matter of whether Capitu's actions are
voluntary or involuntary is open to question. At times her
reactions or expressions seem not to be under control, such as
when she "fez-se cor de pitanga" (chap. xii, p. 741), or when
she "fez-se cor de cera," and exploded with the interjections
against D. Glória, "Beata! Carola! Papa-missas!" (chap. xviii,
p. 747). At other times she shows amazing control over her
emotions and physical reactions, as in her ready responses
when her father almost catches her and Bentinho holding
hands: "—Vocês estavam jogando o siso? [Pádua] pergun-

tou. . . . —Estávamos, sim, senhor, mas Bentinho ri logo, não
agüenta" (chap. xv, p. 474). Or as in her response to her mother
when nearly caught kissing Bentinho: "—Mamãe, olhe como
este senhor cabeleireiro me penteou; pediu-me para acabar o
penteado, e fez isto. Veja que tranças!" (chap. xxxiv, p. 765).
While these events are not in themselves ambiguous, they tend
to contaminate other events at crucial times, making it impossible for us to know whether a given action of Capitu's is an
involuntary indicator, or a controlled signal designed to disguise.

Capitu's crying at Escobar's wake is taken by Bentinho to be a
clear sign that she is in love with the former (a +). Counterbalancing this interpretation, however, are a number of interpretations contrary to the first (b +). Her crying might indicate
a feeling of pity for Sancha and Capituzinha, a realization of the
fleeting nature of life, a sisterly esteem, or any combination of
these emotions. The first of these feelings seems particularly
feasible in view of Capitu and Sancha's close friendship, and
Capitu's empathy for Sancha demonstrated when Sancha was
sick by caring for her to the point of exhaustion (chap. lxxxi,
p. 813).

The chapter "Os braços" (chap. cv, p. 834) contains a subtle
suggestion that Capitu may love Escobar. Bentinho becomes
jealous when he sees the attention Capitu's bare arms attract at
dances. He mentions his disapproval to Escobar, who also disapproves. He then asks Capitu not to appear in public with bare
arms, and for extra authority says Escobar also disapproves of
Sancha's dressing that way. Capitu promptly obeys. But is she
obeying Bentinho or Escobar? Her obedience points in either
direction (a/b).

The narrator presents Capitu's first sight of Escobar as evidence of her fascination with him. Her question, "Que amigo é
esse tamanho?" (chap. lxxi, p. 805), certainly indicates curiosity, a curiosity that might well be taken as "love at first sight"

(a +). But when seen in conjunction with other evidence—that "tudo era matéria às curiosidades de Capitu, mobílias antigas, alfaias velhas, costumes, notícias de Itaguaí, a infância e a mocidade de minha mãe, um dito daqui, uma lembrança dali, um adágio dacolá" (chap. xxxi, p. 762)—her interest in Escobar becomes just one of the many objects of her general curiosity, with no specific amorous suggestion (b +). We are left unsure as to whether this is a special example of her curiosity, or just one of so many others. If the former, it shows cause to suspect Capitu of adultery. If the latter, it may show a poor girl's fascination with rich people's lives, her campaign to become intimate with Bentinho's family, or simple, innocent curiosity—but hardly the beginnings of adultery.

The ambiguity surrounding Capitu's actions inevitably involves the question of her motives, and of her emotional disposition toward her husband. In support of his thesis that he has been betrayed, Bento relates several incidents in which Capitu appears to act almost cruelly toward him. For example, on one occasion she pinches the ego of Bentinho, who is already oversensitive about his manhood, by asking the question, "Você tem medo?" and not specifying exactly what he might be afraid of. After exciting his curiosity, she puts an end to that turn of their conversation, dismissing her question as "maluquice," but not before smiling and saying, "Medroso!" (chap. xliii, p. 776). Just afterwards, she calls him "mentiroso" and threatens to marry another man and ask Bentinho, as a priest, to baptize her first child (chap. xliv, pp. 777–78). Another seemingly cruel action involves her flippantly undoing, "com um enfadamento gracioso e voluntário," the "penteado" received at the hands of Bentinho—a hairdo, we must remember, that has ended in their first kiss, and in Bentinho's mind is directly related to the kiss (chap. xxxiv, p. 765). There is also her refusal to grant a second kiss when asked (chap. xxxvi, p. 768); her turning Bentinho away when he comes to visit (chap. xxxix, p. 770); and her affirming with conviction that Bentinho would make a good priest, when queried by D. Glória in Bentinho's presence (chap. lxv, p. 798). All of these in one light seem to suggest a lack of affection, even a disdain for Bentinho (b − or a +). In another light, however, they point us in the opposite direction. Capitu's "Você tem medo?," her accusation of "mentiroso," and threat of marrying another might be intended as motivating pricks of Bentinho's sensitive ego—an attempt to instill bravery and encourage action by a kind of reverse psychology. The undoing and disparagement of Bentinho's "penteado" is part of Capitu's cover-up of the recently exchanged kiss as her mother enters; her affirmation that Bentinho is a born priest is also part of the cover-up. Her refusal to grant a second kiss, and indeed many of such seemingly cruel actions might be interpreted as simply a part of the inviting-escaping pattern in the behavior of lovers. In short, all of the above incidents, which on the one hand point to a perverse cruel streak in Capitu, might also be viewed as her attempts to seal her love for him by assuring their marriage.

The conclusion that both Capitu and Escobar are dishonest and conniving relies on several bits of evidence. In the case of Escobar, there is the suggestion that he has designs on Bentinho's money. He engages Bentinho in a discussion about arithmetic and asks him as part of an addition problem to tell the rent for each of his mother's properties (chap. xciv, p. 824). Later, he obtains a loan from D. Glória, and there is even a hint that he had thoughts of proposing marriage to her (chap. xcviii, p. 828). There is a rumor that Escobar is guilty of marital infidelity: "Em tempo ouvi falar de uma aventura do marido, negócio de teatro, não sei que atriz ou bailarina, mas se foi certo, não deu escândalo" (chap. civ, p. 833). Once again the narrative itself gives us cause to doubt these suggestions. Escobar must have already had a good idea as to the extent of the Santiago's holdings before proposing the arithmetic problem, because Bentinho had already told him in general terms (chap. xciii, pp. 822–23). The context of the chapter, "Idéias arit-méticas," makes it seem possible that Escobar is interested in the numbers rather than the goods they represent, because he theorizes enthusiastically about the beauty of numbers and is extraordinarily adept at quick figuring (chap. xciv, p. 824). As far as his designs upon D. Glória and his "negócio de teatro" are concerned, the source of these rumors makes them suspect. Prima Justina, source of the former, is suspicious of everyone. In addition, as a companion to D. Glória in her widowhood she is apt to be overly sensitive to any kind of attention shown to D. Glória. The source of the latter allegation is an unspecified rumor; the narrator himself points to its uncertainty: "se foi certo."

Capitu's conniving cannot be denied in many cases. Her obsequious behavior towards D. Glória, with the apparent end of assuring intimacy with the family, attracts the attention of Bentinho, and brings the remark from Prima Justina: "Não precisa correr tanto; o que tiver de ser seu às mãos lhe há de ir" (chap. lxvi, p. 800). We can see her careful planning to avoid Bentinho's becoming a priest, and her psychological manipula-tion of Bentinho through a series of prods to his ego: "—Você? Você entra [no seminário]. —Não entro. —Você verá se entra ou não" (chap. xviii, p. 747). We see her ability to get promises out of Bentinho by appearing to promise everything herself. On the occasion of the "juramento do poço," for example, she promises to marry Bentinho or no one in order to get a firmer promise from him—that he would marry her, come what might (chap. xlviii, pp. 780–81). When Bentinho suspects her of flirt-ing with young men passing by her house, she cries and prom-ises never to go to her window. This promise is a means of extracting a promise from Bentinho, that he will never suspect her again (chap. lxxvi, p. 808). Capitu's talent for feigning is well known to Bentinho, for he is in many cases her partner in the "dissimulação." This trickiness seems even to show in her physiognomy, as evidenced by José Dias' oft-referred-to remark about her "[olhos] de cigana oblíqua e dissimulada" (chap. xxv, p. 754).

Escobar's conniving nature, then, is ambiguous. Clues suggesting this trait are often counterbalanced by contradictory signs. The manipulatory, feigning quality of Capitu is not so much ambiguous as it is vague. We are left with the question of how far that less-than-honest behavior goes. Can the classification of Capitu as a deceiver be as relevant in the context of marital vows as it is in the context of teenage hand-holding? She could conceal a stolen kiss from her mother, but would she conceal one from her husband?

Bentinho seems sure that Capitu lies to him at one point—when she dismisses her question "Você tem medo?" as "nada," but later says, "ouvi falar que lá [no seminário] dão pancada." He calls her lie one of social nicety (chap. xlvii, p. 780). If Capitu would lie to Bentinho to avoid offense, would she do so under more serious conditions? The context does not permit us to know. Bento sees another manipulatory untruth when she cuts their honeymoon short with her frequent mention of their parents, saying "que eles podem estar desejosos de ver-nos e imaginar alguma doença" (chap. cii, p. 832). The concealed truth behind that statement, he says, is her desire to be seen by the world in her new social position. Assuming this conclusion to be correct, can it really help us conclude that Capitu would betray her husband? It suggests that social standing is a major part of Capitu's motivation. Even if that is so, there is not necessarily a contradiction between Capitu's need for social ascension and her loyalty to Bentinho. On the other hand, if she looks outward so soon after marriage she might be even more disposed to find satisfaction elsewhere after a few years. Such questions involve an ambiguity of another order. We have always to ask ourselves whether her deceptive nature applies in

the particular case of adultery (a +), or whether it is too innocent to apply in such a case (a −).

The Role of Point of View

The preceding analysis has been an attempt to outline in
concrete terms the sort of mental balancing act a careful reading of the novel requires. As he comes upon the facts of the
story, the reader is repeatedly required to decide whether a
particular occurrence supports Bento's accusatory interpretation or its counterinterpretation. Or, in the case of relatively
unequivocal data, he is asked to decide whether or not a given
fact is pertinent to the central enigma. A choice is demanded of
the reader because of the dichotomous logic of the depicted
situation. Capitu either betrayed her husband or she did not. It
is logically impossible for her to have betrayed him and at the
same time not to have done so. It is logically impossible for
Ezequiel to have two different fathers. However, the relatively
balanced nature of the textual clues pointing to either hypothesis makes it impossible for the reader to make a confident
choice of either alternative.

As mentioned earlier, we have based our analysis so far upon
the assumption that we can rely upon the indicators in Santiago's narrative. It is natural to begin this way when we are
dealing with any first-person narrator, for we are in effect
obliged in our reading to proceed upon the assumption that the
narrator is telling the truth until we are informed otherwise. In
first-person narratives, it is common for this counterindication
to be achieved by means of irony involving a more or less naive
narrator. The revelation of the narrator's unreliability takes
place behind his back, as it were. However, when the first-
person narrator is a knowing, self-conscious one, we may be
placed in the difficult position of being warned by the narrator
against trusting the narrator. This sort of caveat is of course self-

collapsing—the kind we are exposed to in the famous paradox, when a Cretan tells us all Cretans are liars. In such a case we are encouraged to believe one proposition (that Cretans cannot be trusted) by applying its negation (that Cretans *can* be trusted). Mutual exclusives are thus incorporated into a single imperative statement, and we are left dumbfounded. To trust, or not to trust?

The same sort of situation occurs in *Dom Casmurro*. Santiago encourages our confidence by recounting the details in his case against Capitu—and even a great number of details, as we have seen, that seem to acquit her—with great attention and accuracy. This "escrúpulo de exatidão," as he calls it (chap. 1, p. 782), is counterbalanced by contrary references to his unbridled imagination. We have already seen his admission that he prefers "livros omissos" so that he can fill in the lacunae as he wants with his imagination. In addition, we might recall his fantasy of having the emperor absolve him from attending the seminary (chap. xxix, p. 758); his visions of grandeur about attending a funeral in the family coach (chap. lxxxvii, pp. 817–18); his obsessive jealousy of "algum peralta da vizinhanca," jokingly referred to by José Dias (chap. lxii, pp. 795–96); and his reference to his imagination as an "égua ibera," capable of conceiving by the wind (chap. xl, pp. 772–73) as evidence to reveal a quality within him quite opposite from an "escrúpulo de exatidão." These references are in effect warnings to the reader to be suspicious of the narrator's reliability. It is fascinating to note, however, that at the same time these disclaimers are urging us not to trust Bento, they are urging us to trust him because their revelation is part of the very code of scrupulous exactitude that builds our confidence in his dependability. The matter of *Dom Casmurro*'s point of view, then, is a kind of logical impasse. The thoroughly self-conscious narrator advises us not to trust him. Following his advice involves not following his advice. This ought to remind us of Capitu's remark, "era natural dissimular," which in essence amounts to: "I can lie when I need to, but I'm not lying to you now." Unbelief requires belief, and vice versa.

Critics admitting the ambiguity of *Dom Casmurro* have generally overrated the role of narrative point of view in the creation of that ambiguity.[22] The employment of an involved first-person narrator is only part of the total mechanism for the creation of ambiguity within the novel. A primary ambiguity arises from the selection of the narrative's facts. The narrative structure of *Dom Casmurro* is ambiguous independently of a point of view; that is, the work would be ambiguous even if told in the third person. When point of view enters the picture, we are persuaded on the one hand by the balanced nature of the facts that the narrator is truthful, even to the point of writing a confession (chap. lxix, p. 803), but on the other hand we are asked to believe by the narrator himself that he is either deceitful or deceived. Thus, the matter of point of view acts as a kind of "ambiguity to the second power," compounding the equivocation and confounding the reader whenever the urge to choose begins to take over.

Ambiguity as a Binder of Motifs

Within the structure of the narrative, ambiguity acts as a "binder" of the various units of action. Boris Tomashevsky defines "bound motifs" in narrative as those that are essential to the causal sequence of the story, and "free motifs" as those that are more like appendages and could be removed without a loss of the story's causality.[23] Without going into whether our use of the terms is precisely the use Tomashevsky would make of them, we can see that the reading that does not take sides, that recognizes ambiguity for what it is, accounts for more of the story's motifs as bound motifs than any one-sided reading can. Ezequiel's penchant for imitating others is but a free motif, for

example, if we hold to the "Capitu guilty" reading. However, as
a counterbalancing response to that reading it is integrally
bound to the "Capitu innocent" version. An impartial reading
tells us that this and most other actional motifs in *Dom Casmurro* are somehow bound motifs—not tied to a single underlying story but rather to two intersecting stories. Some motifs
are bound to one, some to another, and some in different ways
to both.

Metaphor and Universal Themes

Even after we have explained the important elements of the
novel's action as part of a system of mutually exclusive propositions, we have a long way to go before explaining the function of
all or even most of the novel's fabric of motifs. So much of the
work's surface texture—"Os vermes," "A ópera," "O *Panegírico
de Santa Mônica*," "Os olhos de ressaca," etc.—appears to
remain unbound by the strictly delimited realm of the story.
There is much more happening in the novel than what goes on
between Bentinho and Capitu. *Dom Casmurro* communicates
meaning through several interrelated codes or levels. We have
concentrated so far upon a code containing a central enigma for
the reader to resolve. Using this concrete, specified code as a
point of departure, the work enters into other realms of meaning, such as the relation of man to the universe, and the relationship between artists (or perceivers of art) and works of art.
The principal mechanism for making such universal and metaliterary statements out of a mere "did she or did she not" is the
device of metaphor. The metaphors and the worlds of meaning
they open to us are, as we shall see, controlled and enriched by
the story of what happens between Bentinho and Capitu.

We can express the first of these metaphorical relationships
with the formula: Bentinho is to Capitu as Man is to Life (the
global term "Life" implies such concepts as the universe,
being, the absolute, meaning, and God).[24]

$$\frac{\text{Bentinho}}{\text{Capitu}} = \frac{\text{Man}}{\text{Life}}$$

The metaphor thus expressed implies likeness, not only between the relationship on the left hand and the relationship on the right, but also between Bentinho and universal man, and between Capitu and the universe. Textual evidence that helps establish any of the equivalences supports the whole equation.

The metaphor of Capitu's "olhos de ressaca" is at the crux of this relationship. Reflecting back upon their mutual eye-gazing, the narrator invokes the muse of rhetoric with the words:

> Retórica dos namorados, dá-me uma comparação exata e poética para dizer o que foram aqueles olhos de Capitu. . . . olhos de ressaca? Vá, de ressaca. É o que me da idéia daquela feição nova. Traziam não sei que fluido misterioso e enérgico, uma força que arrastava para dentro, como a vaga que se retira da praia, nos dias de ressaca. Para não ser arrastado, agarrei-me às outras partes vizinhas, às orelhas, aos braços, aos cabelos espalhados pelos ombros; mas tão depressa buscava as pupilas, a onda que saía delas vinha crescendo, cava e escura, ameaçando envolver-me, puxar-me e tragar-me. (Chap. xxxii, p. 763)

The image of the sea, "fluido misterioso," which both attracts the subject and then threatens dissolution, is itself suggestive of a vast universe. The image of a beautiful woman situated within a threatening ocean ambient is an archetypal image of life itself, of meaning, of the cosmos. The transformation operating in the novel is that the ocean is within the woman, rather than her being within the seascape.

Numerous other references to the sea within the novel reinforce its association with the universe or life: "eu lhe . . . [disse] que a vida tanto podia ser uma ópera como uma viagem no mar" (chap. ix, p. 737); "a salvação ou o naufrágio da minha existência inteira" (chap. xx, p. 751); "[Depois do beijo,] Colombo não teve maior orgulho, descobrindo a América" (chap.

xxxiv, p. 766); "não se navegam corações como os outros mares deste mundo" (chap. xlix, p. 781); "a ilha dos sonhos, como a dos amores, como todas as ilhas de todos os mares" (chap. lxiv, p. 798); "Não confundam purgatório com inferno, que é o eterno naufrágio" (chap. cxiv, pp. 843–44); and "conto aquela parte da minha vida, como um marujo contaria o seu naufrágio" (chap. cxxxii, p. 857).

The metaphoric equivalence of the unsteady relationship between Bentinho and Capitu and a ship's voyage on a troubled sea contributes toward taking *Dom Casmurro* beyond the level of a picture of domestic manners, or a "did she or did she not" mystery, and situating it in the realm of works that inquire into universals. The sea association ties into a traditional body of works from the *Odyssey* to *Os Lusíadas* in which the sea voyage suggests a quest for ideal truths and glory. Bentinho thus carries a suggestion of the archetypal hero, but in a displaced, modernized form. He presents a combination of the weak, petty nonhero who stammers, chews coconut candy, and can't manage to write a sonnet, and the classical hero who takes on the mysteries of the cosmos.

This figurative dimension has its religious proportions as well. Description of childhood play between Bentinho and Capitu has sacred associations: "Arranjávamos um altar, Capitu e eu. Ela servia de sacristão, e alterávamos o ritual, no sentido de dividirmos a hóstia entre nós; hóstia era sempre um doce" (chap. xi, p. 739). If the "doce" can be consistently associated with the idea of spiritual communion, we can say that Bentinho is after such a communion with Capitu when he buys her a "cocada" (chap. xvii, p. 748). When they are married, Bentinho cites to Capitu from the Bible (chap. ci, p. 831). Bentinho's relationship with Capitu is suggestive of the relationship between man and God, and his disaffection with his wife coincides with his disaffection with God. Signs of this separation are Capitu's accusal that Bentinho "não acredita em Deus" (chap.

cxxxviii, p. 862), and Bentinho's not accompanying Capitu and Ezequiel to mass (chap. cxl, p. 863), events surrounding Bentinho's bitter accusal of his spouse. In the beginning Bentinho has a vocation. Through the language of metaphor, his stance before God becomes equal to his stance before Capitu: "Oh! minha doce companheira da meninice, eu era puro, e puro fiquei, e puro entrei na aula de S. José, a buscar de aparência a investidura sacerdotal, e antes dela a vocação. Mas a vocação eras tu, a investidura eras tu" (chap. li, p. 783). Bentinho's vocation is lost. His estrangement from Capitu suggests man's separation from God.

Most scholars have taken it for granted that Machado's world view is presented with consistency, at least in his later works, and that that view is pessimistic or even nihilistic.[25] The view of Casmurro as expressed in the final lines of the novel seems entirely in accordance with such a philosophy:

> E bem, qualquer que seja a solução, uma cousa fica, e é a suma das sumas, ou o resto dos restos, a saber, que a minha primeira amiga e o meu maior amigo, tão extremosos ambos e tão queridos também, quis o destino que acabassem juntando-se e enganando-me . . . A terra lhes seja leve! (Chap. cxlviii, p. 870)

Bento Santiago's view is a strong negation of any truth or value in life. That negation is intimately connected to his affirmation about Capitu and Escobar—"quis o destino que acabassem juntando-se e enganando-me." He accuses not only his wife, but also his life ("o destino") of betraying him. That is the narrator's conclusion, but is it Machado de Assis'? This study has shown that Bento's reading of the facts may be valid or invalid. We must admit the possible inaccuracy of his interpretation. Because Bento's judgment rests on his interpretation of the facts, we must also admit the possibility of a contrary philosophy suggested by the novel. An equally plausible read-

ing, in opposition to that of Bento, encourages us to conclude
that Capitu, while not angelic, is nevertheless faithful to her
husband. The same reading in its more universal dimension
suggests that life may not be a paradise, but it may not be a trap
or an abyss of nothingness either. To use *Dom Casmurro* as
evidence for an outright negation of any positive value in life is
to have made a one-sided reading of the novel, probably based
on a one-sided reading of its ambiguous story.[26] The philosophical dimension is intimately linked to the equivocal drama between Bentinho and Capitu.

I am not attempting here to reexamine Machado's world
view. I am contending, however, that *Dom Casmurro* by itself
appears not to justify an unequivocal assertion of nihilism. If
there is any philosophical generalization to be derived from the
novel, it is more probably a kind of passive pessimism or non-
affirmation. *Dom Casmurro* seems to say that life is not necessarily cruel, nor is it necessarily secure and certain; life is
ambiguous. The silent, mysterious universe incarnate is Capitu, who, when confronted, refuses to justify herself one way or
the other. Any attempt to live affirmatively in such a universe
involves an act of faith—either in the direction of Casmurro's
suspicion or in the direction of trust. In either case we live
dangerously, for we may be wrong. The only risk-free approach
is nonaffirmative living—a kind of repudiation of will. We see a
shadow of this passive approach to life in the novel's encounter
between Bentinho and the leper Manduca. Although en-
livened for a while by his participation in a polemic with Bentinho, Manduca finally dies. Bento sums up the encounter, and
suggests such a passive approach by concluding that in Manduca's case "era melhor haver gemido somente, sem opinar
cousa nenhuma" (chap. xci, p. 821). Machado appears to manage not to "opinar cousa nenhuma," and he does so by invent-
ing a narrative that holds itself perpetually in check.

A Metaliterary Reading

Another important metaphorical relationship creates a meta-literary level of discourse throughout the novel. This relationship may be described by the formula: Bentinho is to Capitu as the reader is to the text.

$$\frac{\text{Bentinho}}{\text{Capitu}} = \frac{\text{Reader}}{\text{Text}}$$

"Reader" may be taken in its most general sense to mean anyone engaged in an act of decoding, and "text" to mean a code in whatever medium (normally, but not necessarily artistic).[27] Because of the metaphoric situation discussed earlier, we actually have a three-part system of equivalence in the novel:

$$\frac{\text{Man}}{\text{Life}} = \frac{\text{Bentinho}}{\text{Capitu}} = \frac{\text{Reader}}{\text{Text}}$$

Through metaphor, the central story of Bentinho's interaction with Capitu is equivalent to the universal process of living, which in turn becomes equivalent to the artistic process of reading. Through mutual equivalence with Capitu and Bentinho, life is a book or some other work to be deciphered, and man in his existential quest is a reader. In fact, very often the metaphors as stated bypass the relation of Capitu and Bentinho. This equivalence is nevertheless always implied. A few examples of metaliterary references in the novel follow: "A vida é uma ópera e uma grande ópera" (chap. ix, p. 737); "Tudo é música, meu amigo. No princípio era o *dó*, e o *dó* frez-se *ré*, etc." (chap. ix, p. 738); "a minha vida se casa bem a definição. Cantei um *duo* terníssimo, depois um *trio*, depois um *quatuor*" (chap. x, p. 738); "antes que ela raspasse o muro, li estes dous nomes, abertos ao prego, e assim dispostos: BENTO/CAP-ITOLINA . . . Padre futuro, estava assim diante dela como de um altar, sendo uma das faces a Epístola e a outra o Evangelho" (chap. xiv, p. 743); "Capitu teve um risinho descorado e in-crédulo, e com a taquara escreveu uma palavra no chão; in-clinei-me e li" (chap. xliv, p. 777); "o destino, como todos os dramaturgos, não anuncia as peripécias nem o desfecho. Eles chegam a seu tempo, até que o pano cai, apagam as luzes, e os espectadores vão dormir" (chap. lxxii, p. 805); "nem tudo é claro na vida ou nos livros" (chap. lxxvii, p. 809); and, "Assim se formam as afeições e os parentescos, as aventuras e os livros" (chap. xcviii, p. 829).

What is the basis of equivalence that allows this metaphorical comparison between our protagonists' interaction, living, and perceiving art? There is in each case a willful search for mean-ing. This is half of the force that sustains the relationship on all levels, and is embodied concretely in the figure of the man Bentinho. The other half is the enigma, without which the search for meaning would remain inert—the archetypal enigma in the concrete form of an attractive woman.

The interaction between Bentinho and Capitu follows an alternating, wavelike pattern of approaching and retreating. Repeatedly, Bentinho is drawn towards her and feels the prom-ise of possession or communion, but then something seems always to push him away. This oscillation of approach and re-treat applies to enigmatic women, and to enigmatic texts as well. Abraham Kaplan and Ernst Kris, for example, describe such a fluctuation in the reader's shift in psychic level between an affective, noncritical response and an intellectual, critical response—a reaction particularly applicable to ambiguous ex-pressions.[28]

Certain images in *Dom Casmurro* seem to act in sympathy with the wave pattern just described. The most important of these is the image of Capitu's "olhos de ressaca."[29] One of the meanings of the ambiguous word, "ressaca" (I will bring up other meanings later), is "tide" or "flux and reflux." Each of the numerous references in the novel to her eyes, and specifically to her "olhos de ressaca," serves to remind us of the oscillating rhythm underlying the work. Even when the context does not justify the tidal denotation, when the "ressaca" is "uma força que [arrasta] para dentro" (chap. xxxii, p. 763), there may be a residual suggestion tying into the rhythmic dimension of the novel. Capitu, life, and the novel each contain a common figurative core, and interact with their respective subjects according to an undulating motion. The image of the sea helps fuse these levels.

On the metaliterary level, *Dom Casmurro* refers not only to literature and art in general, but it also refers to itself. It offers comments about the experience of perceiving all art, *and* the novel itself as a particular piece of *ambiguous* art. The reader's response to ambiguity is ambivalence. Ambivalence, the swaying of the mind between mutually exclusive propositions, is another form of experience that is isomorphic with the wave structure of the novel. However, with ambiguity, there seems to be an added dimension. We may get a glimpse of this dimension by returning to Capitu's "olhos de ressaca." The word "ressaca" is one of those fascinating words that means opposing things.[30] According to the *Novo dicionário da língua portuguesa*, one of its definitions is "refluxo de uma vaga depois de espraiar," which describes a retreating movement. One of its other definitions is "Investida fragorosa contra o litoral, das vagas do mar muito agitado." In this case, rather than retreating, the movement is against the shore. How do we reconcile these mutually exclusive directions? One way is by an oscillating trade-off. This method of reconciliation may be responsible for yet another definition of the word—that of the tidal ebb and flow. First the wave retreats, then advances, then retreats, etc. But what if we impose a restriction that says that both definitions must be effective simultaneously? We must now imagine a wave that retreats and advances at the same time—and we have just such an image when "ressaca" refers, as it often does, to an undertow, that "flow of water at the bottom of a shallow sea in a direction opposite to the surface current produced by the wind" (*Funk and Wagnall's New Standard Dictionary*). The simultaneous coexistence of these opposing waves within the same body of water can be a terrible, destructive natural phenomenon.

Ambiguity is art's undertow. It creates a situation that in effect calls for an advancing wave and a retreating wave in the same space, at the same time. In nature, such a situation is entirely possible, as the undertow attests. In art, the demands of logic can make such a situation impossible: "A natureza é simples. A arte é atrapalhada" (chap. xciv, p. 824). Capitu cannot be both unfaithful and faithful. She must be either one or the other. Yet somehow, her faithfulness and her unfaithfulness seem equally plausible. The effect is quite similar to that of an undertow, for it threatens to annihilate the logical basis that reigns within the book's fictional world.

Bentinho's encounter with Capitu's "olhos de ressaca" thus acquires the dimensions of a bout with utter destruction: "aqueles olhos . . . traziam não sei que fluido misterioso e enérgico, uma força que arrastava para dentro, como a vaga que se retira da praia, nos dias de ressaca" (chap. xxxii, p. 763). The interplay is equally suggestive, through metaphor, of the reader's encounter with an ambiguous text such as *Dom Casmurro*. The mysterious, energetic fluid of enigma draws the reader into the narrative; his assumptions of the work's similarity to real life and solid logic are like a swimmer's muscles made limber and capable after exercise. But at the moment when reason seems most appropriate and necessary, it becomes helpless and seems to flounder. Poised on the edge of a vortex, the reader glimpses an abyss of nothingness, of confounded assumptions, and he recoils.

The abyss, a "hole in the world," seems to be a metaphor for deletion, which is a "space between the sheets" and a "hole in

the text." Deletion invites us to fill in the gap with our imaginations. But with the novel, when we get close enough to do so,
we are nearly overwhelmed with its gaping dimensions. This
"mise en abîme" image occurs a couple of times in the work,
and each time seems to suggest ambiguity's point of vertigo-
producing confusion:

> Percorreu-me um fluido. Aquela ameaça de um primeiro
> filho, o primeiro filho de Capitu, o casamento dela com outro,
> portanto, a separação absoluta, a perda, a aniquilação, tudo isso
> produzia um tal efeito que não achei palavra nem gesto; fiquei
> estúpido. (Chap. xlv, p. 779)

> A leitora, que é minha amiga e abriu este livro com o fim de
> descansar da cavatina de ontem para a valsa de hoje, quer fechá-
> lo às pressas, ao ver que beiramos um abismo.
> Não faça isso, querida; eu mudo de rumo. (Chap. cxix,
> p. 849)

Initially, the reader's response when he encounters a moment of profound ambiguous disjunction seems to be to alter
his hypotheses, in order to accommodate semantic conflicts.
The reader is ambivalent. Before mustering the resolve to ac-
cuse Capitu, Bentinho experiences ambivalence. Appropriately, his mental condition, like the reader's, is concretely
depicted by a physical change in direction: "Quando cheguei a
esta conclusão final, chegava também à porta de casa, mas
voltei para trás, e subi outra vez a Rua do Catete" (chap. cxxvii,
p. 853).

Because of the equitenability of its opposing propositions,
ambiguity seems capable, like the tide, of sustaining indefi-
nitely a shift between opposing directions. This might go on
forever within the reader's mind unless on his own he puts a
stop to it. In moments of profound confusion, the reaction may
be to recoil from the dangers of reading altogether. The novel
suggests just such a solution by advising the reader to throw

away the book: "Abane a cabeça, leitor, faça todos os gestos de incredulidade. Chegue a deitar fora este livro" (chap. xlv, p. 779); and, "A leitora, que . . . abriu este livro . . . quer fechá-lo às pressas" (chap. cxix, p. 849). By sending Capitu away to Europe, Bentinho chooses essentially this same solution. He concludes that she is guilty, and instead of allowing the passage of time to sustain his ambivalence, he makes his charges and forces a separation. By this act, he is able to "fechar o livro às pressas" and "deitá-lo fora" until he is moved to take it up again by writing.

As we mentioned earlier, a willful search for meaning sustains contact between interacting parties on all levels of the novel's significance. Bentinho's absolute conclusion against Capitu is a leap of faith against faith, and prematurely puts an end to his quest for meaning. Another possible reaction to the ambiguous quest, besides leaping for safety to one bank or the other, is a renunciation of will—simply refusing to leap, or to run, or even to walk towards the vortex. By taking this stance (or nonstance) the reader is like a man sitting placidly on the beach watching the waves, without venturing into the water. A powerful image of this attitude is presented in the chapter entitled "Os vermes." Bento, in an enthusiastic search for the origin of a particular idea (a suggestion of man's search for meaning), looks through a library of old books, and goes so far as to inquire of the bookworms:

> Catei os próprios vermes dos livros, para que me dissessem o que havia nos textos roídos por eles.
> —Meu senhor, respondeu-me um longo verme gordo, nós não sabemos absolutamente nada dos textos que roemos, nem escolhemos o que roemos, nem amamos ou detestamos o que roemos; nós roemos. (Chap. xvii, p. 786)

Finally, however, a more heroic approach is suggested: abandonment to the enterprise. "O mar amanhã está de desafiar a gente. . . . Você não imagina o que é um bom mar em hora bravia" (chap. cxviii, p. 848). These words of Escobar suggest the exhilaration of active involvement in the quest. The challenge of the sea points to the challenge of existence, love, the text. A certain promise is suggested in the approach taken by this character who arranges things and accepts challenges.

This alternative, like the others, is brought out by the narrator in one of his digressions: "Amai, rapazes! e, principalmente, amai moças lindas e graciosas; elas dão remédio ao mal, aroma ao infecto, trocam a morte pela vida... Amai, rapazes!" (chap. lxxxvi, p. 817). The imperative "amai" thus expressed is a call to action that extends into all areas of the novel's system of meaning. The promise offered to the active participant in all these areas is a kind of ecstasy or knowledge of the goodness of the universe—"remédio ao mal, aroma ao infecto, . . . vida pela morte."

Active involvement, both in art and in life, seems to provide within the novel an opportunity to transcend the arbitrariness of normal existence. Bento's account of a violin-playing barber whom he came across after brooding on the streets over his suspicions, gives a glimpse of art's transcending potential:

> Quanto ao marido [o barbeiro], tocava agora com mais calor; sem ver a mulher, sem ver fregueses, grudava a face ao instrumento, passava a alma ao arco, e tocava, tocava...
>
> Divina arte! . . . Nunca me esqueceu o caso deste barbeiro, . . . Pobre barbeiro! perdeu duas barbas naquela noite, que eram o pão do dia seguinte, tudo para ser ouvido de um transeunte. Supõe agora que este, em vez de ir-se embora, como eu fui, ficava à porta a ouvi-lo e a enamorar-lhe a mulher; então é que ele, todo arco, todo rabeca, tocaria desesperadamente. Divina arte! (Chap. cxxvii, pp. 853–54)

Such total involvement is a form of ecstasy. All other worldly problems—the normal business of practical life and the reversals of destiny—disappear for a moment. Normal consciousness is annihilated and replaced with another consciousness not of the reasonable world. In *Dom Casmurro* there is a close connection between annihilation and ecstasy. We have seen that connection in Bentinho's encounter with Capitu's eyes. We notice that there is not only a psychological ego-destruction involved in his being swept into her eyes, but also an ecstatic demolition of his impression of time: "Quantos minutos gastamos naquele jogo? Só os relógios do céu terão marcado esse tempo infinito e breve" (chap. xxxii, p. 763). The same suggestion of ecstasy occurs in the case of Escobar's demise. Bentinho's best friend loses his life in an undertow. The undertow is in Capitu's eyes. Therefore, Escobar loses himself in ecstasy with Capitu's undertow eyes. Whether or not they were literally united, Casmurro's use of metaphor brings Escobar and Capitu together in a union that seems destined by nature itself. Capitu is an undertow. Escobar succumbs to an undertow. The suggestion of sexual transport and abandon is unmistakable, but it is an equivocal ecstasy. Is the embrace real or imagined?

When we realize that the undertow refers to the ambiguous work of art, we must also recognize the uncertain promise of artistic ecstasy—a kind of mystical transcendence of daily time and space, afforded to the enterprising reader. Bentinho, prototype of the reader who is deceived or betrayed, never allows himself to come into ultimate contact with Capitu or, by extension, with his "capítulo" or text. At the moment when he is nearest, rather than plunging forward he recoils. Escobar comes to that vortex and keeps going. He is transported by the undertow out of this world and into another, carrying with him the knowledge that is the object of Bentinho's conjecture.

Metaphorically, Bentinho and Escobar represent two contrasting types of readers faced with the "ressaca" of mutually exclusive meanings. Theirs are alternative ways of resolving ambivalence. Bentinho experiences the undertow, but recoils to safer ground. He arrives at a conclusion, through a willing act of faith. Escobar suggests the reader who, finally, gives up the problem-solving mentality, who "succumbs" to the acknowledgment of irresolvability, being transported in a kind of rapture to another level of artistic understanding.

3
Three Versions of
Pedro Páramo

One of the most often mentioned cases of visual ambiguity concerns the question: "Which is the figure in a particular representation, and which is its background?" Edgar Rubin's "reversible goblet"[1] is a familiar specimen of this phenomenon, called "figure-ground reversal" (see fig. 3.1). When we see a goblet in the figure, the space surrounding the goblet is without structure and serves only as a background. But when we perceive the figure as two human profiles facing each other the goblet melts away and becomes but a space between structures.

This chapter will discuss an analogous phenomenon in Juan Rulfo's novel, *Pedro Páramo*. Involved in this "figure-ground reversal" are not two, but three competing structures. Each one motivates its own interrelationship among elements in the novel. The perception of one of these structures seems to require the disappearance of the others, just as with Rubin's figure seeing the profiles requires the disintegration of the goblet, and vice versa.

Ambiguity matters most in a work when tension is created between the opposing propositions. Before beginning a description of these structures in *Pedro Páramo*, we will briefly discuss such a tension-producing factor in the novel, which is usually present in ambiguous texts—what we might call a solution-finding mode. Ambiguous works thrive on the impression that a solution is both possible and necessary. It is the promise of a solution that draws the reader into the text, makes him weigh evidence and encourages him to linger cautiously over the work's language.

Juan Rulfo's novel is the sort of work that encourages resolution, but at the same time seems insoluble. The very first sentence of the novel, uttered by Juan Preciado, is "Vine a Comala porque me dijeron que acá vivía mi padre, un tal Pedro Páramo."[2] With this statement we become aware that the novel involves a quest for someone or something. The sentence also establishes the importance of language and testimony in that search, with the words "porque me dijeron." Right away the epistemological difficulties are made evident. Abundio, the muleteer who accompanies Juan Preciado into Comala, asks, "—¿Y a qué va usted a Comala, si se puede saber?" (p. 8). The phrase "si se puede saber" is on the one hand a polite expression, equivalent to "if I might ask." On the other hand, how-

Fig. 3.1. Rubin's "reversible goblet"

ever, it exposes the essential problem of the quest, with the more literal meaning "if it is possible to know (or find out)." The search will be a challenge, for it involves illusions, dreams, and false hopes. Juan indicates this as he promises his dying mother he will seek out his father, and continues,

> . . . no pensé cumplir mi promesa. Hasta ahora pronto que comencé a llenarme de sueños, a darle vuelo a las ilusiones. Y de este modo se me fue formando un mundo alrededor de la esperanza que era aquel señor llamado Pedro Páramo, el marido de mi madre. Por eso vine a Comala. (P. 7)

The role of equivocation in the quest, especially as it reflects on the unreliability of language, is highlighted in the encounter

between Juan Preciado and Abundio. In the following inter-
change, Abundio is the first to speak:

—¡Váyase mucho al carajo!
—¿Qué dice usted?
—Que ya estamos llegando, señor.
—Sí, ya lo veo. ¿Qué pasó por aquí?
—Un correcaminos, señor. Así les nombran a esos pájaros.
—No, yo preguntaba por el pueblo, que se ve tan solo, como
si estuviera abandonado. Parece que no lo habitara nadie.
—No es que lo parezca. Así es. Aquí no vive nadie. (P. 11)

Twice in the passage, Abundio and Juan fail to "connect" semantically. Abundio's first utterance seems to Juan to be a
curse, something like "Go to hell!" When asked to explain,
however, Abundio says something about going not to hell, but
to Comala. Abundio has previously remarked that Comala is
"en la mera boca del infierno" (p. 9), so there is a vague pe-
jorative connection between seemingly unrelated utterances.
Juan asks "¿Qué pasó por aquí?" meaning "What happened
here?" and Abundio instead answers the question "What
passed by here?" a more literal interpretation of the same
words.[3] Even Abundio's final remark, "No es que parezca. Así
es," calls attention to the fundamental question of appearance
versus essence.

Such equivocations and questions about knowing are essential considerations in an ambiguous work. The first few pages of
Pedro Páramo set the tone for the novel, and in effect instruct
the reader what to expect and how to react (Juan Preciado is a
kind of prototype for the novel's implied reader).[4] The beginning establishes that the work will involve a search for understanding, and that it will be a difficult search full of mistaken
judgments, illusions, failures of communication, and exaggerated hopes. The rest of the novel fulfills the expectations encouraged by the opening scene, by means of ambiguity
appearing in many places and on different levels.

The Near-solid Narrative Structure

The first structure we will discuss—the most obvious one—
is the story of the protagonist Pedro Páramo. This is the novel's
most evident structure not necessarily because it is the most
accessible one, but because by convention novels have a narrative element, and we tend to look for that one first. Actually,
the novel's underlying story requires considerable effort to un-
cover, because of the numerous artistic transformations, including achronological ordering, digressions, and deletions,
which produce the surface representation. Even so, we may
discover a relatively stable story. As Luis Leal has stated, at first
glance the novel "da la impresión de tener una estructura bas-
tante desorganizada, por no decir caótica. . . . Una lectura
cuidadosa, sin embargo revela que, dentro de esa aparente
confusión, hay una ingeniosa estructura, bien organizada y con
una rígida lógica interna."[5]

For Leal, the story line of the tale is "más que sencillo."
Close examination reveals, however, that in certain parts the
story is actually "menos que sencillo." At numerous specific
points, *Pedro Páramo* has an ambiguous story. This ambiguity
has the same features as those which we described earlier in
Dom Casmurro. It involves the coexistence of two or more
mutually exclusive propositions, but differs with respect to its
location. In Machado's novel, we saw that conflicting hypotheses were central, suggesting substantially different interpretations of the story as a whole. In Rulfo's work, ambiguity is
not so central to the narrative; there is really only one story or
underlying structure. However, within that relatively univocal
story there are pockets of ambiguity that defy resolution.

Several of these pockets of ambiguity center around individual characters. Our discussion of the matter begins with the
question of who is dead and who is alive in the novel. The
conventional, worldly means for separating the dead from

the living of course do not apply in the work, because people
who are dead by definition, such as Juan Preciado's mother,
Dolores, can continue talking and moving about (p. 14). The
reader is first faced with the problem of deciding who is dead or
alive. Then the point in time at which characters die becomes
an open question. Here we will analyze the mechanism used to
create this ambiguity, starting with Juan Preciado, and what
Kent Lioret calls the "case of multiple possibilities"[6] concerning his death.

The first explicit indication of Juan's status comes at the point
when after a day and a night in Comala he tells Dorotea that he
has died from lack of air:

> No había aire. Tuve que sorber el mismo aire que salía de mi
> boca, deteniéndolo con las manos antes de que se fuera. Lo
> sentía ir y venir, cada vez menos; hasta que se hizo tan delgado
> que se filtró entre mis dedos para siempre. (P. 61)

Life and death can have their own definitions in fiction; it is
especially evident from *Pedro Páramo* that the state of death is a
matter defined internally by the novel. It is also internally
defined that there is a *distinction* between life and death. The
fact that Juan Preciado talks about dying at a particular moment
implies that he passes from state A to state B, and that there is
an essential difference between the two. On other occasions,
characters stress the necessary distinction between life and
death. For example, upon arriving at Comala, Juan Preciado
asks Abundio about finding lodging, and the latter suggests,
"Busque a doña Eduviges, si es que todavía vive" (p. 13). The
implication is that Juan may stay at Eduviges' place only if she is
alive, and that if she is dead he will have to look elsewhere. Juan
indeed finds Eduviges. She later tries to ascertain whether the
Abundio Juan met on his way to Comala is the Abundio she
knows. Because the one she knows is deaf and the one Juan
spoke with seems to have heard well, she determines that

Juan's acquaintance must not be the same person, and concludes "No debe ser él. Además, Abundio ya murió" (p. 20).
One might well ask why Eduviges is asking about Abundio if he
is dead, but there is still with the last statement a definite
distinction made between life and death. Juan Preciado could
not have spoken to the Abundio Eduviges knows, for he is no
longer alive. The obvious implication is that Juan is alive. Eduviges tells Juan about receiving a visit from Miguel Páramo
some time earlier, in which the youth thought he must be
insane because he could not find his girlfriend's village. Her
reply, "No. Loco no, Miguel. Debes estar muerto" (p. 26),
shows the same rigid thinking oriented toward life and death as
distinct and separate worlds. Miguel cannot find the village
because he now lives in another world. Life and death are
exclusive: that is the hypothesis encouraged by these distinc-
tion-drawing passages. Following such a hypothesis, we can
assume that Dorotea, Donis, and his sister/lover are alive, because they are the ones who bury Juan Preciado (p. 62). Dorotea is only able to join Juan in the grave by dying as she helps
to bury him. Eduviges must be alive, because Juan finds her at
home, talks to her, and she offers him lodging. And Juan is alive
up until his suffocation.

But while this solid life/death dichotomy seems necessary
according to certain textual clues, upon consideration of others
it seems quite impossible. Eduviges, the one most instrumental in establishing the hypothesis of distinctions, is also the one
who most places it in doubt. If Miguel Páramo is dead, if he can
see her, and if she can talk to him, then she must be dead also.
Damiana Cisneros suggests to Juan Preciado that Eduviges *is*
dead: "—¿Eduviges Dyada? —Ella. —Pobre Eduviges. Debe
de andar penando todavía" (p. 37). Following the criteria established, where the dead and the living may communicate, but
only with their own kind, then Juan Preciado, who has talked to
Eduviges, has been dead at least since meeting her. Abundio

may also have been dead, and therefore been the one Eduviges knew (although we still have to wonder about his deafness). Information from the third-person narrator, which Juan Preciado has no knowledge of, establishes the fact that Eduviges truly is dead, that she has committed suicide (p. 34). Juan would then seem definitely to have been dead long before he thinks he died. But what about Dorotea and the others, who were witness to his death and burial? Perhaps they are dead along with everyone else. But that would present us with the strange case of the dead burying the dead, which might be an acceptable hypothetical teaching device in the New Testament but hardly fits into the rigid distinctive system the novel seems to call for.[7]

The dichotomy between life and death and the incongruous arrangement of textual evidence put the reader in a quandary. Who is dead and who is alive? If they are all dead, at what point did they die? One possible reaction on the part of the reader is to come to regard the distinctions as meaningless, to maintain that the rigid logic of the life/death dichotomy does not exist.[8] On the one hand, the novel with its impossible interface between life and death seems to lead us in this direction. But on the other, it induces us to sustain rigid logic and seek a solution. We have seen that from the beginning of the work, the theme of the quest for knowledge is established. In a first-person narrative involving this theme, because the reader has only as much knowledge as the protagonist he is practically obliged to become a participant in the search for knowledge.[9] *Pedro Páramo* has a mixture of first-person, third-person, and objective points of view. Perhaps the reader's impulse to take part in the quest is ambivalent because of this mixture. But it seems that as long as Juan Preciado is actively involved in the effort to know about the status (alive or dead) of his acquaintances, of himself, and of his father, we as readers tend to be searching also. Juan goes about his quest with a high degree of seriousness and intensity: "¿Está usted viva, Damiana? Dígame, Damiana!" (p. 46). The intensity of this search seems to rub off onto the reader, so that instead of seeing the textual situation as a set of hopeless contradictions, he sees them as a set of clues apparently incongruous, but quite possibly soluble. As he weighs certain possibilities he momentarily forgets their corresponding impossibilities. Characters seem to move back and forth between the world of the dead and that of the living.

In matters other than life or death, we find characters in other pockets of ambiguity. One of these is Susana San Juan, the woman whom Pedro Páramo has loved since childhood. There is a suggestion that Susana has an incestuous relationship with her father.[10] Fulgor Sedano, Páramo's foreman, mentions seeing them after an extended absence from Comala, and Pedro asks:

—¿Han venido los dos?
—Sí, él y su mujer. ¿Pero cómo lo sabe?
—¿No será su hija?
—Pues por el modo como la trata más bien parece su mujer.
—Vete a dormir, Fulgor. (P. 85)

The conversation between Susana San Juan and her father, Bartolomé, in which Bartolomé tells her Pedro wants to live with her, is a rich specimen of ambiguity:

—¿De manera que estás dispuesta a acostarte con él?
—Sí, Bartolomé.
—¿No sabes que es casado y que ha tenido infinidad de mujeres?
—Sí, Bartolomé.
—No me digas Bartolomé. ¡Soy tu padre! . . . Le he dicho que tú, aunque viuda, sigues viviendo con tu marido, o al menos así te comportas; he tratado de disuadirlo, pero se le hace torva la mirada cuando le hablo, y en cuanto sale a relucir tu nombre, cierra los ojos. Es, según yo sé, la pura maldad. Eso es Pedro Páramo.

—¿Y yo quién soy?
—Tú eres mi hija. Mía. Hija de Bartolomé San Juan.
En la mente de Susana San Juan comenzaron a caminar las
ideas, primero lentamente, luego se detuvieron, para después
echar a correr de tal modo que no alcanzó sino a decir:
—No es cierto. No es cierto. (P. 88)

Obviously Bartolomé does not approve of Susana's living
with Pedro Páramo. But why? Is it because Pedro Páramo is "la
pura maldad," or because Susana is a sort of wife to Bartolomé?
The words, "Le he dicho que tú aunque viuda, sigues viviendo
con tu marido, o al menos así te comportas," are equivocal.
They might mean that Susana lives with her husband in the
sense of maintaining loyalty to him and being unavailable to
others. But it also might suggest that Susana is living in a quasi-
marital relationship, that her father is her "marido." Susana's
calling her father by his first name might suggest more of a
husband-wife relationship than a father-daughter one. Surely
Bartolomé is sensitive about her addressing him in such a familiar way. Bartolomé tries to use his parental authority to get her
to stay with him: "Tú eres mi hija. Mía. Hija de Bartolomé San
Juan," and after some time Susana says, "No es cierto." Is she
reflecting upon her role as a "wife" to Bartolomé when she says
this? Is she going crazy? Is she correcting her father's judgment
of Pedro Páramo? Different contexts seem to shift back and
forth from prominence to unimportance, figure to ground.[11]
There is a suggestion that Bartolomé abuses his daughter
physically as well as sexually. Again describing his conversation
with Pedro Páramo, Bartolomé says,

Así que te quiere a tí, Susana. Dice que jugabas con él
cuando eran niños. Que ya te conoce. Que llegaron a bañarse
juntos en el río cuando eran niños. Yo no lo supe; de haberlo
sabido te habría matado a cintarazos."
—No lo dudo.
¿Fuiste tú la que dijiste: no lo dudo?
—Yo lo dije. (P. 87)

To what does Susana's comment "No lo dudo" refer? If it has reference to Bartolomé's "te habría matado a cintarazos," then Susana seems practically to be calling her father a child beater. However, it might also refer to Pedro Páramo's statement that he and Susana swam together in the river as children, and carry no suggestion of abuse.

This passage makes us wonder if there is not an ambiguous suggestion of physical abuse a few pages later, when a flashback depicts Bartolomé lowering Susana by a rope into what seems to be a mine shaft: Susana "Estaba colgada de aquella soga que le lastimaba la cintura, que le sangraba sus manos" (p. 94). Bartolomé insists that there is money and gold at the bottom of the shaft, but instead Susana finds a skeleton:

> Entonces ella no supo de ella [la calavera], sino muchos días después entre el hielo, entre las miradas llenas de hielo de su padre.
> Por eso reía ahora.
> —Supe que eras tú, Bartolomé. (P. 95)

At the point in the novel when Susana says, "Supe que eras tú, Bartolomé," she seems to have already gone insane. So the most obvious interpretation of the remark is that it is a demented one: Susana has confused the cadaver at the bottom of the shaft with her father, who is holding the rope at the other end. But might there be some lucidity in the remark after all? Might she be realizing that there was no treasure to be found, but rather that she was simply being played with by her father? His "miradas llenas de hielo" suggest something sinister. Might he even be responsible for the skeleton? The text supplies data to suggest alternative hypotheses, but not enough to substantiate any hypothesis satisfactorily.

A further bit of ambiguity surrounding Susana concerns her obsession with Florencio. Because every reference to Florencio within the novel is filtered through Susana San Juan (part of her monologue from the grave, her dreams, or her interior monologue while alive), and because we know that Susana has gone insane, it is impossible to establish definitely even if Florencio exists.[12] There are a number of propositions that suggest themselves. Surely as far as Susana is concerned, Florencio has been her lover (pp. 100, 104) and has died (pp. 96, 104). One possible hypothesis is that Florencio was Susana's husband. We have already seen that Susana's father refers to her as a widow (p. 88).

However, we have also seen that because of the suggestion of incest between Bartolomé and Susana there is reason for wondering if she really is a widow. Bartolomé might be obliquely referring to himself as her "husband"—"sigues viviendo con tu marido" (p. 88). A second possibility, then, is that Florencio is in Susana's mind a purified version of her father. We know that Bartolomé dies at about the time Susana moves in with Pedro Páramo. Páramo orders Fulgor Sedano to "desaparecer al viejo en . . . regiones adonde nadie va nunca" (p. 89), and Justina, a servant at Páramo's, announces Bartolomé's death to Susana. When upon receiving a visit of consolation from Padre Rentería, Susana thinks, "Ya sé que vienes a contarme que murió Florencio" (p. 96). It seems quite possible that she is considering Florencio and her father to be one and the same.

Still another possibility is that Florencio is a purified, idealized conception of Pedro Páramo, held by Susana since childhood, who perhaps "dies" when Susana is forced to face the real Pedro. We hear a monologue by Susana in her grave, recounting her bathing naked in the sea with an unidentified man (pp. 99–100). The tone is consistent with her sensual, idyllic evocations of Florencio, so we assume she is referring to him. But this monologue reminds us of Pedro Páramo's having told Bartolomé "Que . . . ya conoce a Susana. Que llegaron a bañarse juntos en el río cuando eran niños" (p. 87). Therefore, through the motif of the "baño" there is a connection suggested between Pedro and Florencio as well. Susana's deceased husband? An idealized representation of Bartolomé or Pedro Páramo? Perhaps an entirely nonexistent being based on scraps of remembered experience with various individuals? The reader seems encouraged by the work's coincidental motifs to advance conjectures. But the incompatibility of suggested propositions, plus the paucity of additional detail makes any sort of well-founded conclusion impossible.

The character Abundio, who appears at the beginning and end of the novel, provides yet another locus of ambiguity within the narrative structure. One question that must be asked in his case is: "Is Abundio one character, or are there two Abundios?"[13] The Abundio who demands money from Pedro Páramo at the end of the work is clearly named Abundio Martínez (pp. 125–26). The one who accompanies Juan Preciado into Comala at the beginning might be named Abundio Martínez, but then again might not. "—¿Y cómo se llama usted? — Abundio —me contestó. Pero ya no alcancé a oír el appellido" (p. 13). Here a distinction on the basis of last names is made to seem possible, but at the same time, no distinction can be made. Likewise, we are encouraged to make a distinction on the basis of deafness or hardness of hearing. The Abundio at the end of the work is supposed to be hard of hearing. Doña Inés, who gives Abundio liquor at her son's bar, speaks to Abundio shouting, because "Abundio era sordo" (p. 123). The Abundio with whom Juan Preciado speaks seems to have had no problem hearing. On that basis, it would seem that there are two different Abundios. However, it is not quite that simple. The question becomes not only whether there are two different Abundios, but whether either is really hard of hearing. Doña Inés' conversation with Abundio illustrates:

¿Qué es lo que te trae por aquí tan de mañana?
Se lo dijo a gritos, porque Abundio era sordo.
—Pos nada más un cuartillo de alcohol del que estoy necesitado.

—¿Se te volvió a desmayar la Refugio?
—Se me murió ya, madre Villa. Anoche mismito, muy cerca de las once. Y conque hasta vendí mis burros. Hasta eso vendí porque se me aliviara.
    —¡No oigo lo que estás diciendo! ¿O no estás diciendo nada? ¿Qué es lo que dices? (P. 123)

On the basis of this passage, if anyone seems hard of hearing it is Doña Inés, just as Juan Preciado is the one who has problems hearing when he talks with Abundio. Abundio seems to hear well. But then, Doña Inés *is* shouting so she can be heard. Perhaps she can only hear herself, or is hard of hearing as well. When Abundio Martínez arrives at the Media Luna, he seems to have no trouble hearing Damiana Cisneros, but then, she is shouting also:

. . . los gritos de Damiana se oían salir más repetidos, atravesando los campos: "¡Están matando a don Pedro!"
    Abundio Martínez oía que aquella mujer gritaba. No sabía que hacer para acabar esos gritos. No les encontraba la punta a sus pensamientos. Sentía que los gritos de la vieja se debían estar oyendo muy lejos. Quizá hasta su mujer los estuviera oyendo, porque a él le taladraban las orejas, aunque no entendía lo que decía. (P. 126)

This passage gives the impression both that he hears and that he is deaf. He hears the shouts, feels that even the dead must hear them (his wife is dead), but at the same time does not understand what the shouts are saying. One or two Abundios? Deaf or not deaf? Once again we see that the text provides us with indices for making a determination, but that the data that is to help us decide is equivocal, so we can make no determination.

    Critics who have commented on the matter have generally agreed that Abundio kills Pedro Páramo.[14] We know that Abundio stabs someone, but are we sure it is Páramo? Here is the crucial passage:

—¡Ayúdenme! —[Abundio] dijo—. Denme algo.

Pero ni siquiera él se oyó. Los gritos de aquella mujer lo dejaban sordo.

Por el camino de Comala se movieron unos puntitos negros. De pronto los puntitos se convirtieron en hombres y luego estuvieron aquí, cerca de él.

Damiana Cisneros dejó de gritar. Deshizo su cruz. Ahora se había caído y abría la boca como si bostezara.

Los hombres que habían venido la levantaron del suelo y la llevaron al interior de la casa.

—¿No le ha pasado nada a usted, patrón? —preguntaron.

Apareció la cara de Pedro Páramo, que sólo movió la cabeza.

Desarmaron a Abundio, que aún tenía el cuchillo lleno de sangre en la mano:

—Vente con nosotros —le dijeron—. En beun lío te has metido. (P. 127)

Here we see the image of Abundio's bloody knife. Surely he has stabbed someone. But there are apparently two persons he might have stabbed. Abundio is obviously distraught by Damiana's yells, and gropes for "qué hacer para acabar con esos gritos" (p. 126). Suddenly her shouting stops, she drops to the ground and has to be carried into the house. Abundio might well have stabbed Damiana. But how about Pedro Páramo? His men try to find out about his safety, and all the text gives us on the matter is the marvelously vague "Apareció la cara de Pedro Páramo, que sólo movió la cabeza" (p. 127). At other moments, Damiana screams, "¡Están matando a don Pedro!" (p. 126) and Páramo says to himself, "Se que . . . vendrá Abundio con sus manos ensangrentadas a pedirme la ayuda que le negué" (p. 128). These comments, while perhaps suggesting that Abundio kills Páramo, are by no means unequivocal. Why would Damiana say "están" if she were referring to Abundio alone? Pedro Páramo's comment seems like a premonition, but can it be taken as evidence of an accomplished fact?

All of these ambiguities—Florencio's identity, Abundio's

crime, the existence of one or two Abundios, Susana San Juan's relationship to her father, etc.—are like cracks in an aged sculptured monument that efface an area here, create a dubious form there, but leave the more general representation intact. Generally speaking, the ambiguities belong to the more dispensable and superficial *free motifs*, rather than to the *bound motifs* that make up the essential underlying structure of the narrative.[15] How Pedro Páramo dies may be equivocal, but the more important fact, that he dies as the culmination of a gradual self-induced corruption, remains unambiguous. This narrative structure, tracing the rise and decline of the *cacique* Pedro Páramo, and the generally tragic effect his life has on others, is stable, and readers can readily agree on the general story and themes of the work. The portion of the novel concerning Juan Preciado's search for his father, which occupies a rather large part of the concrete, surface structure of the novel and is one of the most ambiguous parts, is rather marginal as far as the deep structure or abstract story is concerned. Again, if one is concerned only with the fact that Juan Preciado dies, all the ambiguity concerning when, where, and how is of little importance.[16] But the work seems designed to direct our attention to these details, these small fissures and gaps that come into view as we take a closer look at the monument. We weigh possibilities in the choice of words. We consider both literal and figurative meanings of statements. We find alternative referents for certain statements. And, when our initial attempts to solve the enigmas are frustrated, we tend to return to the text for another try.

The Expressionistic Reading

In the previous chapter, while noting the applicability of some general notions of linguistic theory to the study of the novel, I mentioned that a novel and a sentence can be considered analogous in certain respects. One of these is that both the novel and the sentence have a form of syntax. Just as we can consider the connections among phonemes, morphemes, and words in the formation of a sentence, we can analyze the connections between units of narrative in a novel, and thereby gain some notion of a syntactic structure for the work.

The idea of breaking a work down into minimal narrative units is not a hard one to grasp when we consider *Pedro Páramo*, for graphically the job has already been accomplished. The narrative consists of about sixty-five short segments, separated by white spaces. We need not go into whether these sections qualify as minimal narrative units by the various rather technical definitions developed by specialists in the morphology of narrative. For our purposes, each block may simply be considered as one unit, which might be compared to a word for purposes of discussing syntax.

Syntax involves the concatenation of elements. In grammar, subjects are connected to verbs, verbs to objects, modifiers to nouns or verbs, etc. The chief syntactic forces acting in a novel are causality and chronology (practically always acting harmoniously). *Pedro Páramo*, like other narrative works, has a syntax based on these forces. But its narrative syntax does not correspond with the segments' syntax in the concrete medium of the novel. For example, consider the essential narrative material of the novel's first four segments: (1) Juan Preciado meets Abundio on his way to Comala; (2) Juan, now in Comala, is invited into a woman's house; (3) Juan arrives at Comala and takes leave of Abundio; and (4) Juan learns the woman is Eduviges and enters her house. The narrative syntax of these segments is one, three, two and then four, rather than the order in which they are artistically presented. Considering the work's chronology of events, these segments actually belong near the end rather than at the beginning. The work's underlying story has a syntax determined by causality and order in time, but through a series of artistic transformations its representation has frequent inversions in this order. Reading the novel involves reworking its surface syntax—mentally putting the segments of narrative back into their causal sequence. Hugo Rodríguez-Alcalá compares the novel's structure to that of a mosaic, "un mosaico de numerosísimas teselas. Y estas teselas debe el lector mismo ordenar, o, mejor, reordenar, a fin de componer las figuras musivas en forma completa e inteligible."[17] This narrative-based ordering, which emphasizes Pedro Páramo's drama and deemphasizes Juan Preciado's, is one version of the novel's syntax. However, it is not the only one. In competition with this ordering, a series of repeating elements constructs a network among the narrative segments that tends to be equally as persuasive as a syntactical system, but not always compatible with the causal, temporal linking. Specifically, we refer to the technique of tying contiguous segments together by means of a common word, phrase, image or motif. Following are several examples of this type of concatenation, all occurring not within, but rather between segments. Usually, but not always, the concatenated elements occur near the end of one segment and the beginning of the next:

1. "—Iré. Iré después" (p. 15), and "Ya voy, mamá. Ya voy" (p. 17).
2. "Y tu madre se fue" (p. 23), and "El día que te fuiste" (p. 24).
3. "Había estrellas fugaces" (p. 33), and "Había estrellas fugaces" (p. 34).
4. "En este cuarto ahorcaron a Toribio Aldrete" (p. 37), and "levantó el acta contra actos de Toribio Aldrete" (p. 37).
5. "¡Vaya!" (p. 38), and "¡Vaya!" (p. 39).
6. "me respondió mi propia voz" (p. 47), and "Y las voces" (p. 47).
7. "salió la estrella de la tarde, y más tarde la luna" (p. 57), and "Volví a ver la estrella junto a la luna" (p. 58).

8. "nubes ya desmenuzadas por el viento" (p. 57), and "Las nubes deshaciéndose" (p. 58).
9. "el golpear de la lluvia" (p. 65), and "gruesas gotas de lluvia cayeron" (p. 65).
10. "a una le cierran una puerta" (p. 70), and "Llamaron a su puerta" (p. 70).
11. "Vete a descansar" (p. 79), and "Estoy acostada" (p. 79).
12. "¿No lo sabías?" (p. 88), and "¿Sabías, Fulgor . . . ?" (p. 89).
13. "la lluvia sobre las hojas de los plátanos" (p. 93), and "la lluvia, . . . rodando sobre las hojas de los plátanos" (p. 93).
14. "Comala seguía anegándose en lluvia" (p. 95), and "La lluvia" (p. 95).
15. "eras tú, Bartolomé" (p. 95), and "¿Eres tú, padre?" (p. 96).

These repeated motifs provide another basis for the connection of segments. We are urged to link segments because of their concatenating words, images, or phrases, rather than because of their causal relationship. Approximately half of the time, there is no conflict between story-based syntax and the chains of elements we have mentioned. There are several groups of segments in the surface representation of the novel that belong together, insofar as the story is concerned. In these cases, both syntactical systems act together. Example number seven, featuring the words "había estrellas fugaces," links a segment in which several men converse during the night of Miguel Páramo's burial, and a segment in which Padre Rentería recriminates himself for "selling out" to those who support him financially. The padre's meditations are also related to Miguel Páramo's burial. In example number thirteen, the words about rain falling "sobre las hojas de los plátanos" link segments that are also chronologically linked, because both have to do with Susana San Juan's bedridden delirium.

In several other cases, however, the syntax of repetitive elements is in direct opposition to the syntax of causality and chronology. Example number one links Juan Preciado's meeting with Eduviges and Pedro Páramo's bathroom reverie about Susana San Juan. Number two creates a link between Eduviges' account of Dolores' leaving Pedro Páramo, and a conversation between Pedro and his grandmother. And number ten involves the connection of a dialogue between Juan Preciado and Dorotea in their graves, and the arrival of Miguel Páramo's body to the Media Luna estate.

These two syntactical systems—the system of narrative causality and the system of element concatenation—urge two incompatible readings of the novel. Both accentuate the duality between the novel's surface texture and its underlying content or story. On the one hand, *Pedro Páramo* urges us, through a sort of reader's quest, to piece together the narrative elements so as to arrive at a comprehension of the narrative content. It is possible to apprehend the work's story, but only through a reordering of the narrative units as they appear on the surface. In order to perceive the story as a solid, firmly comprehensible structure, one must impute a certain fluidity to the artistic discourse so that it can be reordered. The novel thus lends itself to a representational reading. When we follow the representational urge we perceive the novel's deep structure as being solid, rigid, and demanding, while of necessity the novel's surface structure must be malleable and accommodating, perhaps even transparent, more like a liquid than a solid (see chapter 2 for a discussion of narrative's surface and deep structures).

But the surface structure makes demands of its own. The system of concatenating elements, both when it harmonizes with the syntax of the story and when it acts against it, provides strong motivation *not* to reorder the segments, but rather to apprehend them in the order presented in the novel itself. When one is oriented towards this highly formal syntax, he perceives the *surface* of the novel as the more rigid and de-

manding side of the dichotomy. The requirements of causality
and temporality must lose something; the deep structure becomes the more fluid, transparent, accommodating structure.
With this sort of reading the representational aspect of the
novel becomes faded and distorted. Rather than a sharply defined representation, what emerges is the *expression* of a much
more subjective sort of reality.

An expressionistic reading does not necessarily refer to ex-
pressionism as a school or movement, although in many respects *Pedro Páramo* conforms to the norms of the movement.
For our purposes, an expressionistic reading is one that takes
account of literary discourse as expression per se, rather than as
a depiction of something else. Concentrating on the expression
means giving legitimacy to the novel "as is," as an individual
communicative act. It means ignoring that "otherness" which
the expression is about.[18]

The story-centered reading and the expression-centered
reading are in a kind of figure-ground relationship. As with
Rubin's goblet/profiles figure, we cannot perceive both at once.
While all narratives feature the duality of surface structure and
deep structure, of story and expression, not nearly so many
force this sort of ambiguity between the two. Most feature a
more or less transparent expression that does not call attention
to itself. But *Pedro Páramo*, particularly because of its conflicting syntactical systems, is different. Story and discourse each
call attention to themselves, and each distracts from the other.

It is interesting that *Pedro Páramo* at one time had another
provisional title—*Los murmullos*.[19] The difference between
these titles suggests the dichotomy between the novel's expressionistic and representational readings. Rulfo was perhaps himself ambivalent about whether his novel was a story about
Pedro Páramo, or rather a collection of poetically expressed
impressions of some scarcely definable subjective reality. Convention dictates one title for one work; obviously Rulfo chose

his. But perhaps it was an arbitrary choice. The novel might just as appropriately been called *Los murmullos*. Both titles stand for something essential to the work, and both perhaps fail to be entirely satisfactory as labels for the totality of the work.

To recapitulate our discussion of ambiguous syntax and the opposing readings it engenders, we may pretend that there are actually two different novels—one called *Pedro Páramo* and one called *Los murmullos*. Contrasting these two novels will give us an idea of the mutually exclusives that are somehow coexistent in one novel.

Pedro Páramo	*Los murmullos*
1. Represents objective conditions.	1. Expresses subjective impressions.
2. Reader must reorder narrative segments.	2. Reader need not reorder narrative segments.
3. Has a syntax based on causality, chronology.	3. Has a syntax based on a chain of formal elements.
4. Surface structure is fluid, giving way to the demands of the story.	4. Surface structure is solid, demanding attention to its form.
5. Deep structure is solid, because of the rigid demands of the story.	5. Deep structure is fluid, because the story gives way to the demands of formal discourse.

Rulfo's novel is somewhere in between *Pedro Páramo* and *Los murmullos*. The experience of reading the work seems to be one of hesitation, of going and coming, between the two. Both are demanding, but neither is completely satisfying. For example, just when we feel we are succeeding in piecing together the story, we come across the mysterious narrative segment (pp. 27–28) wherein a mother announces to her son, "Han matado a tu padre." We learn several pages later (p. 71) that the

episode involves Pedro Páramo and his mother, but at this point
we cannot tell who the son and mother are, because, as is
typical, no names appear. For lack of character identification,
and because so many men are killed in the novel, our story-
based syntax breaks down. It at first seems that the segment
might connect to any number of segments, or that it might
connect to none. The final line of the segment, "¿Y a ti quién te
mató, madre?" is a nonsequitur. It has little to do with what is
represented, but does contain evocative power. This unworldly
question jars us loose from perceiving predominantly the story,
and makes us savor its anguished, nonsensical expressiveness.
Pedro Páramo disintegrates at such moments, and we begin
reading *Los murmullos*. At other times, however, *Los murmullos* disintegrates as well. We follow the repetitive cadence
of images, words, and phrases. The concatenation of discursive
elements carries us along through one segment after another,
but at critical points, the concatenation terminates. In these
gaps, the persuasive force of the story is allowed to take over,
and as it does so, the rocklike surface structure turns to liquid.

The image just employed ought to remind us of an arresting
image in the novel, where Juan Preciado finds himself in bed
with Donis' sister/lover: "El cuerpo de aquella mujer, hecho de
tierra, envuelto en costras de tierra, se desbarataba como si
estuviera derritiéndose en un charco de lodo" (p. 61). This is
only one of numerous images sprinkled throughout the novel in
which a relatively rigid structure disintegrates into something
nondescript, less-rigid, or even nonexistent: "Y [los hombres]
se disolvieron como sombras" (p. 33); "mis manos tenían que
haberse hecho pedazos estrujando su desesperación" (p. 80);
"El cadáver se deshizo en canillas; la quijada se desprendió
como si fuera de azúcar" (p. 95); and Pedro Páramo "dio un
golpe seco contra la tierra y se fue desmoronando como si fuera
un montón de piedras" (p. 129).

On the other hand there are several images where a soft or

formless structure acquires rigidity. For example: "La voz sacude los hombros. Hace enderezar el cuerpo" (p. 27); "Aclaraba el día. El día desbarata las sombras. Las deshace" (p. 53); and "Por el camino de Comala se movieron unos puntitos negros. De pronto los puntitos se convirtieron en hombres" (p. 127). These frequent images of disintegration and integration harmonize with the competing structures of the novel shifting between exigent rigidity and lax fluidity. Likewise, they suggest the waxing and waning of the reader's will as he grapples with conflicting propositions, alternately experiencing the promise of solution and the frustration of irresolution.

The Structure of Chiasmus

As if these two rival modes of apprehending the novel were not enough, there appears to be yet a third structure that demands our perceptive attention. *Pedro Páramo* seems to be structured upon a system of dual motifs that causes the first half of the novel to mirror the second half, in reverse.[20] Consider table 3.1; each number in the table appears twice, and refers to a pair of textual details that will be outlined shortly. The numbers are distributed horizontally according to the page numbers upon which the signified motifs occur. The vertical distribution is an arbitrary, equal spacing between numbers, which facilitates our seeing the chiasmus. Following are descriptions of the textual details represented by the numbers:

    1a.   Dorotea advises Juan Preciado to make Pedro Páramo pay for his paternal neglect: "exígele lo nuestro. Lo que estuvo obligado a darme y nunca me dio . . . El olvido en que nos tuvo, mi hijo, cóbraselo caro" (p. 7). Juan begins to seek out his father after his mother's death.

    1b.   After his wife's death, Abundio, apparently another of Pedro's neglected sons, seeks out his father and demands

Table 3.1: Chiasmatic Motifs

Page 7	30	50	70	90	110	129
1a						1b
2a					2b	
3a					3b	
4a						4b
5a				5b		
6a					6b	
	7a				7b	
	8a			8b		
	9a				9b	
	10a				10b	
	11a			11b		
	12a			12b		
		13a		13b		
		14a	14b			

Motifs

financial help (pp. 125–27). He is in effect "cobrando el olvido en que Pedro lo tuvo."

2a. Abundio remarks, "Bonita fiesta le va a armar" (p. 8), when Juan says he is going to see his father.

2b. The people of Comala literally "arman una fiesta" after Susana San Juan dies (pp. 120–21).[21]

3a. Abundio appears briefly at the novel's beginning (pp. 7–12).

3b. Abundio (perhaps a different one) appears briefly at the novel's end (pp. 123–27).

4a. Eduviges invites Juan Preciado to eat, and he responds, "—Iré. Iré después" (p. 15).

4b. Damiana Cisneros offers to bring Pedro Páramo his lunch, and he says, "Voy para allá. Ya voy" (p. 129).

5a. Susana San Juan is depicted at the bottom end of an "hilo," flying a kite (p. 16).

5b. Susana appears at the bottom end of an "hilo," lowered by her father into a mine shaft (pp. 94–95).

6a. Pedro Páramo mentally evokes the departure of a loved one, supposedly Susana, with the words, "El día que te fuiste entendí que no te volvería a ver" (p. 24).

6b. Pedro Páramo says to himself, "Hace mucho tiempo que te fuiste, Susana" (p. 122), and mentally evokes the moment of her departure.

7a. Eduviges converses with Miguel Páramo, her secret lover, through a window. Later Eduviges says, "Y cerré la ventana" (p. 26).

7b. Damiana sees Pedro Páramo climbing through a window to Margarita, his secret lover. Then Damiana "Cerró la ventana" (p. 110).

8a. In bed, Pedro awakens, and "Hace endurezar el cuerpo" (p. 27). He learns that his father has been killed (p. 28).

8b. Susana gets out of bed, "Endurezó el cuerpo" (p. 93), and receives word that her father has died.

9a. Padre Rentería resists giving the final blessing to Miguel Páramo's soul at his funeral mass; finally, he gives the blessing (pp. 29–30).

9b. Padre Rentería tries to give last rites to Susana, but she resists; the padre does not pronounce the final blessing (p. 119).

10a. Several men, walking home to retire for the night, discuss Miguel Páramo's death (pp. 32–33).

10b. Two women, walking home to retire for the night, discuss Susana San Juan's approaching death (pp. 115–17).

11a. Pedro Páramo has Fulgor Sedano arrange for his marriage to Dolores Preciado, so as to be rid of debts (pp. 40–41).

11b. Pedro Páramo has Fulgor Sedano arrange for Bartolomé's "disappearance" so that Pedro can live with Susana San Juan (p. 89).

12a. A young man tries to persuade a woman named Chona to run away with him. Chona resists, saying her father needs her (p. 49).

12b. Susana San Juan and her father discuss Pedro Páramo's proposal to live with Susana. Her father resists (pp. 87–88).

13a. An incestuous relationship is depicted between Donis and his sister (p. 54).

13b. An incestuous relationship is suggested between Susana and her father (p. 85).

14a. Juan Preciado lies down with Donis' sister (p. 61).

14b. Dorotea lies down (in the grave) with Juan Preciado (p. 65).

The motifs in the first part of table 3.1 appear in the order they are introduced in the novel. It will be observed that the order of their counterparts is not in precise reversal. However, their approximate conformity to the pattern of chiasmatic reversal is visible. What seems clear enough is that there is an echoing pattern involving certain actions by characters, in which the first and second halves of the novel duplicate each other. The point of division for the pattern is the moment at which Juan Preciado becomes conscious of his death—the same point generally acknowledged by critics as a structural halfway mark for the novel. The paired motifs mentioned are probably not all of those involved in this pattern. In most cases, the pairs are notable for their differences as well as for their similarities. For example, the point of equivalence between 1a and 1b is "requiring Pedro Páramo (as father) to pay." Points of difference are that in one case, Juan Preciado seeks out Pedro at his mother's death, while in the other, Abundio seeks him out at his wife's death. The complementary nature of these differences is often apparent. By virtue of these pairs of similarities and differences, various characters at these points act as doubles of each other.[22]

Some ambiguity is endemic to the pattern of chiasmus. Its halves are equivalent to each other, yet they are also non-equivalent, because their order is reversed. The perception of chiasmus requires the mind to go in opposing directions. The reader proceeds without hesitation to the crux, but then he must read forwards and backwards at the same time—forwards to take in each new motif, and backwards to compare that motif with its earlier counterpart. All of this works against the traditional linear reading of the work, and in addition calls into question whether the second half duplicates the first, or whether it is the first half that duplicates the second.

Chiasmus as a structure involves a return to the point of origin. In *Pedro Páramo,* this structure harmonizes with the frequently expressed theme of return—Juan Preciado's and Abundio's return to their father, Susana San Juan's return to Comala, man's return to the earth through death, etc., and highlights the liberal sprinkling of verbs like "volver" and "regresar" one finds in the novel.

In many other respects, however, the chiasmatic structure is in disharmony with the other structures. The weighing of differences and similarities that is required with nearly every set of paired motifs causes the reader to perform a reduction that discards irrelevant differences. We find emerging from this analysis not so much the *qualities* that characterize the individuals and context of each single motif, as we find the *quantities* that are held in common after these differences have been peeled away. The pattern emerges only by virtue of these quantitative cores. Appropriately, the term "chiasmus" itself derives from the word *chi*, the symbol "χ" which is so often used to stand for a mathematical quantity. A reading of *Pedro Páramo* in which characters and situations are but part of an χ-like form is one that emphasizes the abstract, almost mathematical pattern at the expense of other more concrete considerations.

This third reading of the novel has a figure-ground revers-ibility with the other two. The chiastic pattern takes elements from Juan Preciado's frustrated search as well as elements from Pedro Páramo's story, and causes the multitude of other ele-ments in the novel not directly related to the pattern to drop into the background. Thus, most of the narrative details, as well as most of the texture of the transformed expression are con-signed to nonstructured background status. The narrative reading is essentially linear and chronological as is the expres-sionistic reading with its concatenation of elements. The chiastic reading is also linear, because it proceeds in a fixed order from one motif to the next. But at the same time it appears to be nonlinear and achronological, because it ends up where it started. To the extent that it is nonlinear, the chiastic reading excludes the other two readings of the novel.

Like the narrative and expressive structures we have exam-ined, the structure of chiasmus is not completely convincing. We need only look at its graphic representation to see that it is an imperfect, slightly vague form. Towards its vertex and its ends it is relatively solid, but in the middle regions it seems to begin melting away. The question of whether a particular motif belongs to the pattern must frequently be posed, because in addition to the repetitive pattern of chiasmus and that of con-catenation, there are more random repetitions and leitmotifs that echo through the novel.

The reader who looks for possibilities in *Pedro Páramo* will find at least three attractive readings that can be alternately postulated. But the careful reader who seeks a satisfying solu-tion to the novel's ambiguity will be frustrated. As we men-tioned earlier, there appears to be an implied definition of the reader within the novel, and that reader (as a counterpart of the character Juan Preciado) is a searcher for such solutions. On the one hand we are encouraged to join in the search, and on the other, we are frustrated. Just as Juan Preciado tries to knock on a door but winds up knocking "en falso" (p. 13), the reader is often given to expect that he is about to hit upon some solid structure, only to find because of the imperfection of the structure itself and because of other competing structures, that there might be nothing solid there after all.

Juan Preciado's search ends in frustration; he never finds his father. It might be noted as well that frustration is a common denominator for a good many of the novel's characters. Pedro Páramo is frustrated in his desire to possess Susana San Juan, Dorotea in her need for a child, Padre Rentería in his quest for integrity, Bartolomé in his search for gold and silver, and so on. As with the main characters, so it is with the reader.

Another common denominator among most, if not all, of the characters is that they are dead. Perhaps the reader must also succumb, in the sense that reading is defined as solving something, but there can be no positive solution. He might waver between possible solutions, as if to linger somewhere between life and death. Insisting on the validity of a partial reading, the reader might make it appear from a limited perspective that he is alive and well. But if the structures to be resolved are truly ambiguous, the concept of a reader as a solution-finder must eventually falter and crumble.

4
Cien años de soledad's Unending End

Fiction, which is untrue by definition, may nevertheless meet standards of esthetic truth. The reader apprehends this truth as a sense of fulfillment, a feeling of the work's stability or conclusiveness—its fidelity not necessarily to some outside reality, but rather to its own design. As Barbara Herrnstein Smith shows in her book, *Poetic Closure,* the work's ending is often an important factor in creating this sense of truth. What she says here about poetry may apply equally well to fiction: "The devices of closure often achieve their characteristic effect by imparting to a poem's conclusion a certain quality that is experienced by the reader as a striking *validity*, a quality that leaves him feeling that what has just been said has the 'conclusiveness,' the settled finality, of apparently self-evident truth."[1]

In the chapter containing this statement, Smith discusses several structures or devices of closure,[2] which happen to be found in Gabriel García Márquez' novel *Cien años de soledad.* What she calls *predetermination*—when the form or occurrence of something in the ending has been previously implied and is consequently expected by the reader—is a significant feature of the novel's ending. *Cien años de soledad* keeps most of its promises. For example, when it depicts the birth of the final member of the Buendía family, and bestows upon him a pig's tail,[3] it fulfills the foreshadowing in the beginning of the book when Úrsula, fearing the deformity in her offspring, refuses for a time to have relations with her cousin/husband, José Arcadio Buendía (pp. 24–26). When the entire city of Macondo and the last of the Buendía family are consumed by an "huracán

bíblico" in the end, there is a fulfillment of an early prophetic
vision in which Melquíades "creyó encontrar una predicción en
sus papeles sobre el futuro de Macondo. Sería una ciudad . . .
donde no quedaba ningún rastro de la estirpe de los Buendía"
(pp. 52–53).

According to Smith, conclusive closure is also fostered by the
use of parallelistic structures. The final half of the parallelism,
particularly in the case of antithesis, encourages a sense of
completeness. *Cien años de soledad* as a whole has been said to
have such a structure, apparent in the rise and fall, construction
and decomposition, and expansion and contraction in the saga
of the Buendía family and of Macondo.

The device of *unqualified assertion* is another means of creating the impression of a solid ending, according to Smith. *Cien
años de soledad*'s closing words—"que todo lo escrito en . . .
[los pergaminos de Melquíades] era irrepetible desde siempre
y para siempre, porque las estirpes condenadas a cien años de
soledad no tenían una segunda oportunidad sobre la tierra"
(p. 351)—surely are an unqualified assertion, and seem to encourage a feeling of authority and finality through their prophetic tone.

Considering these features of closure, one might be led to
conclude that the novel has a strong, definitive ending and that
as a whole it can be considered to have a ring of truth, conclusiveness, or authority. My thesis in this chapter is that such
is not the case. Rather than ending with the ring of truth, the
novel concludes with an unending wave of ambiguity. The
seemingly authoritative voice that announces the novel's *Göt-
terdämmerung* is an equivocal one. *Cien años de soledad* ends
not on a note of utter and absolute verity, but rather on a note of
utter uncertainty. This novel, like a war or a basketball game, is
in essence dependent on its ending. Its inconclusive conclusion tends to be a kind of anti-ending, causing us to return to
the text rather than put it down, and to subject it to renewed
scrutiny from different angles of view.

Three Incompatible Facts

The ambiguity results from the confluence of three facts immediately observable by the reader. Two of them are part of the world that is represented by the novel. One involves the fictional, represented world and, as we shall see, the medium that represents as well. The first of these facts is the existence of a manuscript written by the gypsy prophet Melquíades, who, as we learn early in the book, "pasaba horas y horas garabateando su literatura enigmática en los pergaminos que llevó consigo y que parecían fabricados en una materia árida que se resquebrajaba como hojaldres" (p. 68). Pages of his "escritura impenetrable," when read aloud, "parecían encíclicas cantadas" (p. 68). Various members of the family try their hand at reading the manuscript after Melquíades leaves it in the family's custody. It is not until many pages (or years) later, that we learn, facing the end of the book, about the true nature of the manuscript. Aureliano Babilonia discovers

que en los pergaminos de Melquíades estaba escrito su destino. Los encontró intactos, . . . y no tuvo serenidad para sacarlos a la luz, sino que allí mismo, de pie, sin la menor dificultad, como si hubieran estado escritos en castellano bajo el resplandor deslumbrante del mediodía, empezó a descifrarlos en voz alta. Era la historia de la familia, escrita por Melquíades hasta en sus detalles más triviales, con cien años de anticipación. La había redactado en sánscrito, que era su lengua materna, y había cifrado los versos pares con la clave privada del emperador Augusto, y los impares con claves militares lacedemonias. La protección final . . . radicaba en que Melquíades no había ordenado los hechos en el tiempo convencional de los hombres, sino que concentró un siglo de episodios cotidianos, de modo que todos coexistieran en un instante. Fascinado por el hallazgo, Aureliano leyó en voz alta, sin saltos, las encíclicas cantadas que el propio Melquíades le hizo escuchar a Arcadio, y que eran en realidad las predicciones de su ejecución, y encontró anunciado el nacimiento de la mujer más bella del

mundo que estaba subiendo al cielo en cuerpo y alma, y conoció
el origen de los gemelos póstumos que renunciaban a decifrar
los pergaminos no sólo por incapacidad e inconstancia, sino
porque sus tentativas eran prematuras. (Pp. 349–50)

The manuscript, then, is a detailed account of the Buendía
family, covering one hundred years of its history as if it all
occurred contemporaneously.

The second fact represented in the fictional world of the
novel, at the end of the account, is a devouring wind:

Entonces empezó el viento, tibio, incipiente, lleno de voces del
pasado, de murmullos de geranios antiguos, de suspiros de
desengaños anteriores a las nostalgias más tenaces. . . . Aureliano . . . no sintió . . . la segunda arremetida del viento,
cuya potencia ciclónica arrancó de los quicios las puertas y las
ventanas, descuajó el techo de la galería oriental y desarraigó
los cimientos. . . . Macondo era ya un pavoroso remolino de
polvo y escombros centrifugado por la cólera del huracán
bíblico, cuando Aureliano saltó once páginas. . . . Sin embargo, antes de llegar al verso final ya había comprendido que
no saldría jamás de ese cuarto, pues estaba previsto que la
ciudad de los espejos (o los espejismos) sería arrasada por el
viento y desterrada de la memoria de los hombres en el instante
en que Aureliano Babilonia acabara de descifrar los pergaminos. (Pp. 350–51)

The third fact involved in the ambiguity is not as explicit as
the two just mentioned. Apprehending it involves an inference
by the reader. However, the text practically orders the reader
to make this inference. That fact is that the text of *Cien años de
soledad* and Melquíades' manuscript are equivalent. We are
prompted to assume this equivalence because of numerous
parallels between the description of Melquíades' manuscript
and the text we are about to finish reading. Both texts cover one
hundred years of time. Melquíades' technique of concentrating
"un siglo de episodios cotidianos, de modo que todos coex-

istieran en un instante" (p. 350), seems to parallel the curious cyclical treatment of time in our text, as exemplified in its opening sentence: "Muchos años después, frente al pelotón de fusilamiento, el coronel Aureliano Buendía había de recordar aquella tarde remota en que su padre lo llevó a conocer el hielo" (p. 9). As Aureliano Babilonia discovers in the parchments' references to Arcadio, the most beautiful woman in the world ascending to heaven body and soul, the twin boys, and even to himself, we are convinced of the identity of his text with our own because we remember having read the same things. Certain details may not match exactly with what we have read, such as the fact that the "encíclicas cantadas" were predictions of Arcadio's death or the prematurity of the twin's attempts at translating the parchments. However, because of the ambiguous nature of the narration, an indirect discourse, we cannot tell whether these details are actually contained in the manuscript or whether they are Aureliano's reflections as he reads.

As strong as evidence for the equivalence of the manuscripts seems to be, it can be nothing but an illusion. We know all the while that *Cien años de soledad* has actually been written by the Colombian, Gabriel García Márquez. But it is no more of an illusion than the first two facts mentioned. The mind has a talent, and in fact a need, for perceiving representations as if they were not representations of reality but rather a meaningful reality in themselves. That mental capacity for projecting a sense of reality upon representations—Coleridge calls it "the willing suspension of disbelief"[4]—is responsible for our being willing to accept the proposition that the text we are reading can be written by a character within our narrative. We accept this with belief equal to that with which we accept any other textual motif. The only difference about the fact of the sameness of Melquíades' book and ours is that it loops between the world of the represented and the world of the representing agent. We will see that this twisted connection is instrumental in the novel's ambiguous conclusion.

The interaction of these three phenomena, verifiable by the reader through his interaction with the text, creates an impossible but unavoidable relationship among them. We may diagram this relationship using a truth table similar to those employed by Shlomith Rimmon in her discussion of the concept of ambiguity:[5]

	1	2	3	4
manuscript	T	T	T	F
storm	T	F	T	T
novel	T	T	F	T
logical validity	F	T	T	T

The term "logical validity" refers to the reasonability, the sense of plausibility, of the relationship depicted in the numbered columns. To say that the manuscript, the storm, or the novel is true is for our purposes equivalent to saying that it exists. Considering column one, to say that the manuscript, the storm, and the novel all exist is logically invalid. Because the storm appears to destroy everything in Macondo, including the manuscript, and because the manuscript is responsible for the existence of our text, the manuscript cannot have been destroyed without creating a value of "F" or nonexistence, for the text. Therefore, we say that the logical validity of "T T T" for manuscript, storm, and novel is false. In the case of column two, we could have a logically valid relationship by positing the nonexistence of the storm. In these circumstances, the manuscript would be enduring, and therefore could plausibly be equivalent to the novel. By assuming the nonexistence of the text, as in column three, we have another valid combination. Because there is nothing for the manuscript to be equal to, the storm can destroy the manuscript without any contradicting evidence getting in its way. Likewise, the nonexistence of the manuscript as in column four would provide for a logically valid situation, because blow as it might, the storm could not affect the existence of the text. There are other possible valid combinations, such as the nonexistence of all, or of two out of three. These are not included in the table because the nonexistence of two involves no interaction among elements.

To illustrate better the interdependence of manuscript, storm, and novel as an ambiguous structure we will draw a comparison in figure 4.1 with the impossible figure by Penrose and Penrose, introduced in chapter 1. The novel and the draw-

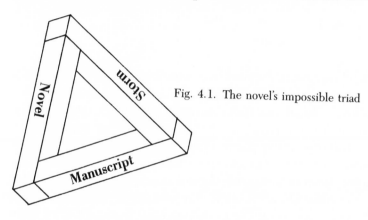

Fig. 4.1. The novel's impossible triad

ing are remarkably similar in a couple of respects. In both cases, there is a crisis of perspective. Is the point of view of the drawing from below the figure or above it, from the right side or the left side? Is the point of view of *Cien años de soledad* from within the narration or from without? In both cases also, there is what might be called a "short circuit"—a connection that by conventional or logical laws should not occur. The impossible drawing is not ambiguous at all if we simply eliminate one of the connections as seen in figure 4.2.[6] By the same token, if we block the storm from destroying the manuscript, or somehow ignore the connection between the manuscript and the text of

Cien años de soledad, we as readers once again stand on solid ground with respect to the novel. But if we follow the signs in the direction they point us, if we allow ourselves to suspend our disbelief, we perceive in the ending of the novel a self-consuming, self-restoring reality. We accept the parallels between Melquíades' parchments and the text we ourselves have been reading. Realizing that all books come from manuscripts, we begin to believe that our book is a product of the manuscript, not bothering about the details of how this might come to pass. We detect the growing hurricane, and begin to see that

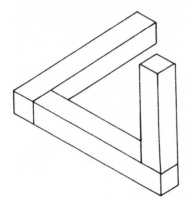

Fig. 4.2. The "impossible object" made possible

it is going to eliminate everything in Macondo. We relish the esthetic truth, the finality, and grand style with which everything ends. But at the final moment, when we have allowed ourselves to become convinced that "las estirpes condenadas a cien años de soledad no [tendrán] una segunda oportunidad sobre la tierra" (p. 351), the very reality of the representation forces us to direct our attention to the text. We are reminded that the manuscript seems to equal the text. The manuscript has just been consumed before our minds' eyes. Therefore, the text should be nonexistent. The text, which has until now been a window through which to view Macondo, loses its transparency as Macondo is blown away. We perceive its white pages and black letters and become aware that the text has endured, for we hold it in our hands. We discover that we can no longer believe the part about the storm, which is part of the reality of Macondo, because the manuscript could not possibly have been destroyed. Or, perhaps we should not believe the part about the manuscript, because without it the storm could exist unhampered. But why should we disbelieve one part of the represented world on the basis of another part of the represented world? We are placed again in the situation described in chapter 2 of having to believe in order to disbelieve. The representation is like a Cretan warning us not to trust Cretans. In this case, however, there is a way out. We can accept the coexistence of the storm and the manuscript, and deny the existence of the text. The object we are holding is but an illusion, and because we are holding it and can feel its texture and weight, *we* must therefore be an illusion. That conclusion is apt not to seem satisfactory for long, so we start over where we began. We discover that what is "irrepetible desde siempre y para siempre" (p. 351) is also "repetible desde siempre y para siempre."

The Ending and the Critics

By using the editorial "we" to refer to the reader of the novel I do not mean to suggest that there is a community of readers, all in complete agreement. A survey of criticism on *Cien años de soledad,* especially that concerning its ending, bears this out. Some of the best critics have sensed the logical contradictions at the end of the novel, but have had difficulty accounting for them explicitly. As a consequence, they have offered a variety of approaches to explaining the novel's ending.

Critics admitting the equivalence of the novel and Melquíades' manuscript have found themselves in an especially difficult spot. One approach to this analytical problem has been to write criticism reflecting the contradictions of the work, that is, criticism that is itself contradictory and ambiguous.[7] Another approach to the problem has been to "transcend" the circular logic of the ending, by concluding that the work is, in the final analysis, fiction.[8] This acknowledgment of the illusion is a typical response of readers sensitive to the novel's motifs that cannot logically coexist, yet seem to do so anyway. It corresponds to column one of the truth table introduced earlier, and amounts to the reader's saying that if the manuscript is true, the storm is true, and the text is true, then the situation is false, or, in other words, an illusion. Directing one's attention to illusion as such is the triumph of reason over what Plato called the "lower reaches of the soul."[9] Plato was referring to the human tendency to advance theories and predict meaning without recourse to measurement or other empirical validation. A name often given to the movement against this tendency is "esthetic distancing," the ability to see the artifice in art. *Cien años de soledad* seems to appeal to the lower reaches of the reader's perceptive capacity in order to bring about a detached, intellectual response. Acceptance of the represented reality leads to rejection of the same. This sort of distancing in the reader's response is perhaps easier to talk about than to achieve in practice. A moviegoer easily forgets about the presence of the screen and projector once the theater's lights go out and the film begins. Most members of our society would be hard put to make themselves think about a movie as a two-dimensional image for very long while they are watching one. Experiments with three-dimensional films and synchronized smells in cinema have not been well accepted, probably not because of expense or impracticality, but simply because they are not necessary. The viewer, even with such infidelities as black-and-white images and subtitles, has all he needs to slip into another world.

Though perhaps not as strongly, the represented world of prose exerts the same kind of pull upon the imaginative impulses. Perhaps the word "pull" is even a bit inaccurate, because usually there is not a resisting force, as the word implies, but rather a kind of complicity between the work and the reader. By picking up a novel, the reader accedes to certain conventions. He agrees to let the internal realism of the work direct his imagination. When readers say of a good book, "I could not put it down," what they might just as well say is that for a while there was a well-kept agreement between the work and the reader to act as if there were no book to put down.

Considering this rather strong impulse to preserve the illusion unnoticed, it should not be surprising that readers have used their imaginative resources to preserve the internal plausibility of *Cien años de soledad*. As we mentioned earlier, the stability of the representation can be preserved if one of the impossible triangle's connections is somehow broken. That result is apparently what some critical interpretations have sought to achieve. One critic, for example, decides that the storm must have destroyed everything in Macondo *except* Melquíades' manuscripts.[10] Another concludes that his manuscripts and the novel are not equivalent.[11]

It is possible to imagine the separation of manuscript and text, and of manuscript and storm, because while it indicates the connectedness of these elements, the text does not do so explicitly. The novel supplies us with details about Melquíades' manuscript that parallel many features of the novel itself. However, the text does not say directly that it is a translation of the manuscript. Similarly, the novel supplies us with enough details to imagine the hurricane obliterating everything outside Aureliano Babilonia's room, and even shows the plaster starting to fly off the room's interior walls, but it does not unequivocally say that the storm devours the manuscript. Textual details lead the imagination in a definite direction, but they stop just short

of supplying a conclusion. There is an ever-so-slight gap in the
novel's seemingly connected lines. Because of our perceptive
capacity for anticipating meaning, we normally have no problem filling in the gap so that the connections seem entirely real.
Certain disconnected visual configurations practically ask to be
perceived otherwise, as the following illustration (fig. 4.3) from
Gombrich shows.[12] It is difficult not to integrate the uncon-
nected black shapes into connected letters. *Cien años de soledad*'s vague connections are no doubt similar to this visual
image. In both cases the observer is persuasively invited to fill
in what is missing. The difference with the novel is that the
connections seem more than necessary when considered sepa-
rately, but then seem impossible when we consider them together. The critics' positions mentioned above represent
several logical attempts by readers to deal with a situation that
cannot be logically dealt with. Resisting the apparent connectedness of text and manuscript or storm and manuscript
provides a sense of surety. However, the storm, text, and manuscript demand in their own right to be connected. We seem to
gain a place on terra firma through assuming an intellectual
aloofness by which a novel is a novel and nothing else. However, the force of convention and our very contact with the
novel argue convincingly that we see not a novel, but rather life
in the pages before our eyes. The illusion continually deconstructs itself and reconstructs itself. A sense of esthetic satisfaction is the dividend awaiting the reader at the end of most
works—the result of a sort of contract in which reader and work
fulfill certain conventional expectations. But upset expectations are an essential part of *Cien años de soledad*'s ending.
That feeling of "settled finality, of apparently self-evident
truth," which Smith shows an ending may provide, is both
confounded and encouraged.

The reader of *Cien años de soledad* is not allowed the satisfying, tension-releasing resolution that lets him put away the

work. He is given reason to expect a definite resolution, but is suddenly fooled, and encouraged to approach the ending again. The novel's conclusion, which at first seems to end everything, is instead the source of an eternal return.

IMAGE   Fig. 4.3. Reader-supplied connections

How the Novel Defines Itself

So far we have proposed the reader's reactions on the basis of alternatives logically possible given certain textual circumstances. Because the novel's ambiguity has a fairly definite structure, the possibilities it suggests seem likewise to be finite and predictable. It would seem safe and worthwhile to discuss the reader's reaction on this basis alone. However, *Cien años de soledad* affords us another means, rich in detail and recapitulation, for apprehending its ambiguity and the accompanying response of the reader. This dimension becomes available as we realize that the novel repeatedly refers to itself.[13] One of the metaphors traditionally employed to describe the representational properties of art has been the mirror.[14] Like a mirror, art offers us images that imitate the world. The same can be said of García Márquez' novel. No matter how exaggerated or fantastic its account becomes, there is always something there that seems a faithful imitation of the Latin American world. However, the novel is not simply a mirror of the world, for that world it creates is also a mirror of the novel. Just as Macondo is "la ciudad de los espejos (o los espejismos)" (p. 351), *Cien años de soledad* is the novel of mirages and mirrors.[15] Their reflective pattern is not a simple one, however. The novel creates the eternal reflexivity of two mirrors placed face to face—an image found within the work as "dos nostalgias enfrentadas como dos espejos" (p. 339), or as twins who seem to be an "artificio de espejos" (p. 151). The novel imitates a world which imitates the novel. When mirrors are aimed at each other in this manner, any intervening object is multiplied as an infinity of images, each a different size. So it is with *Cien años de soledad*. We cannot say whether the ambiguous structure starts in the world or in the work of art, but the structure is repeated practically infinitely. The novel's structure reflects the behavior of the characters, and the structure of the characters' behavior reflects the novel. The repeated similarity is not exact, either with self-reflecting mirrors or with the novel. Facing mirrors repeat the same image with a variation of size. The novel echoes the same essential structures, with an endless permutation of names, settings, or motives. Understanding this reflective repetition, by which characters and circumstances define the novel, is yet another way of learning about the novel's ambiguity and the reader's corresponding response. The book in effect teaches us how to read it.

Readers in Macondo

Depiction of the act of reading is perhaps the most obvious way in which the novel defines itself. Macondo is full of readers. It is easy to see that the reading of Melquíades' manuscript may act as a definition for reading the novel, for as we have seen, the novel and the manuscript seem to be equivalent. The parchments are filled with "signos indescifrables" (pp. 62–63, 68). They are called "literatura enigmática" (p. 68) and their tendency is to attract readers by some irresistible force, at the same time frustrating their interpretations. For example, "José Arcadio Segundo se dedicó entonces a repasar muchas veces los pergaminos de Melquíades, y tanto más a gusto cuanto menos los entendía" (p. 265). Besides drawing in the reader, the manuscript, as the preceding passage shows, tends to induce the reader to "repasar muchas veces." The resistance to unequivocal interpretation, the enigma that draws but frustrates the reader, and the repeatability of readings are all qualities that characterize the novel according to our analysis.

Examining motifs slightly further removed in their connection with the novel itself, we note that references to other manuscripts or written messages seem also to mirror the work. Near the end of the novel, the old Catalonian bookseller is seen writing a manuscript that resembles the novel's contradictory nature: His "fervor por la palabra escrita era una urdimbre de respeto solemne e irreverencia comadrera. Ni sus propios manuscritos estaban a salvo de esa dualidad" (p. 337). Alfonso, one of the bookseller's young admirers, loses a portion of the manuscript in a bordello. The bookseller's remark, "que aquel era el destino natural de la literatura" (p. 337), suggests the self-effacing aspect of the novel's ending. As with the novel, there are misleading and contradictory written messages. Pietro Crespi, the suitor of first Rebeca and then Amaranta, receives a letter announcing the imminent death of his mother. He rushes to her home, only to find she is in good health and has traveled to see him in Macondo (p. 76). The letter Amaranta Úrsula writes to her husand, Gastón, is "una carta de verdades contradictorias" (p. 342). While Aureliano Buendía is fighting a civil war, numerous missives circulate about. The result: "empezaron a recibirse noticias contradictorias de la guerra" (p. 127). All such representations of ambiguous texts, may describe literature in general, but seem also to reflect upon the novel.

The image of Aureliano Segundo "reading" the *Encyclopaedia Britannica,* besides etymologically echoing the novel and the Sanskrit manuscript (enciclopedia—encíclicas cantadas—novela cíclica), represents also the reading of *Cien años de soledad,* particularly with respect to the reader's essential function, explained earlier, of attempting to predict or project meaning. Aureliano, who reads no English,

convirtió el dirigible [de la enciclopedia] en un elefante volador
que buscaba un sitio para dormir entre las nubes. En cierta
ocasión encontró un hombre de a caballo que a pesar de su
atuendo exótico conservaba un aire familiar, y después de
mucho examinarlo llegó a la conclusión de que era un retrato
del coronel Aureliano Buendía. (P. 273)

It is possible to generalize still further, and to consider any
act represented within the novel of interpretation or searching
for meaning as a variation of the reader-text paradigm. This
attitude allows us to see the image of the novel and its reader in
numerous interpersonal transactions, and in encounters between individuals and the world. Gerineldo Márquez courting
Amaranta, perceives her heart as some impenetrable text—
"aquel corazón indescifrable" (p. 142). During the period when
numerous inventions are imported, the people of Macondo in
their reactions are like readers responding to the novel: "la
gente de Macondo no sabía por dónde empezar a asombrarse"
(p. 194). Their ambivalence in the face of these marvels echoes
the oscillating response of the reader as he is confronted with
an impossible combination of realities:

> Era como si Dios hubiera resuelto poner a prueba toda ca-
> pacidad de asombro, y mantuviera a los habitantes de Macondo
> en *un permanente vaivén* entre el alborozo y el desencanto, la
> duda y la revelación, hasta el extremo en que nadie podía saber
> a ciencia cierta donde estaban los límites de la realidad. (P. 195;
> my emphasis)

Another such echo of the reader's reaction is found in the trial
of the fugitive banana magnate, señor Brown. When confronted with proof from the prosecutors that the defendant is
señor Brown, and then with proof from the defending attorneys
that he is not señor Brown, the townspeople experience a "delirio hermenéutico" (p. 256).

On this general level, that of the interactions between people and objects, the distinctive voice of the novel echoes toward infinity. It would be tedious and unnecessary to indicate all the cases in which characters and things imitate the novel's structures. Nevertheless, a few salient examples of important aspects are called for.

The Short Circuit

The foundations of logic, of perspective drawing, of electronics, and of many other pursuits depend upon keeping certain elements separate from each other. As we saw earlier, the ambiguity of *Cien años de soledad* arises from the "illegal" connection[16] of things that ought to be kept separate—the totally devouring storm, the manuscript, and the novel. As an analogy of this short circuit in visible form, we offered the model of the impossible three-dimensional triangle. Several motifs, themes, or images in the novel repeat this same structure, and can be seen as reflections of the novel. The most important of these seems to be the theme of incest[17]—the illicit connection par excellence. The sexual inclinations and behavior of the Buendías are a continual process of "buscarse por los laberintos más intricados de la sangre" (p. 350), which threatens to create a short circuit in terms of genealogy. The possibilities wreak havoc with one's sense of kinship, as is shown when Aureliano José "oyó contar a alguien el viejo cuento del hombre que se casó con una tía que además era su prima, y cuyo hijo terminó siendo abuelo de sí mismo" (p. 132). The Buendía line ends as the novel ends, by turning back upon itself; the broken sexual taboo mirrors the novel's broken logical taboo.

The civil war carried on by Aureliano Buendía has a similar structure. Consistency and logic demand that war be conducted by irreconcilable parties representing different interests. Such is not the case with this particular war. The notions of liberalism and conservatism, supposedly tensions underlying the conflict, become hopelessly confused. The following incident is one of many indicative of the failure to keep opposing interests in opposition:

> [Era] una situación política tan confusa que cuando [el coronel Aureliano Buendía] ordenó restaurar la torre de la iglesia desbaratada por un cañonazo del ejército, el padre Nicanor comentó en su lecho de enfermo: "Esto es un disparate: los defensores de Cristo destruyen el templo y los masones lo mandan componer." (P. 119)

The image of opposing generals playing chess (p. 130) further suggests the confusion of supposedly irreconcilable elements. Several years before this, José Arcadio Buendía refuses to play checkers, because he "nunca pudo entender el sentido de una contienda entre dos adversarios que estaban de acuerdo en los principios" (p. 78). The converse can be said about the amicable chess matches of Colonel Buendía and General Moncada: one can never understand the sense of an accord between two adversaries who are in disagreement upon principles. All this contributes to an impression of "la incertidumbre, del círculo vicioso de aquella guerra eterna" (p. 146), and it all reflects the structure of the novel.

The image of Aureliano Buendía's dream does the same: "aquel sueño recurrente tenía la virtud de no ser recordado sino dentro del mismo sueño" (p. 228). Logically, dreams should be remembered *outside* the time of dreaming. The failure to separate the time of dreaming from the time of remembering is a logical merry-go-round.

Úrsula's resorting to the classic liar paradox, "No me creas lo que te digo" (p. 96), when she talks to her tree-tied husband is another case of the illegal connection. The statement that a particular person is lying should be made by someone besides that particular person. Otherwise, the logic collapses upon

itself and puts the listener in a position of hopeless ambivalence, because disbelieving requires believing and vice
versa. We have already seen how this same phenomenon operates with respect to the novel's ending.

Even minute details suggest the structure of the short circuit. Remedios' dying, poisoned by her own blood (p. 80); Rebeca's sucking her thumb (pp. 44, 292); and José Arcadio's
cannibalism (p. 84) are but a few of the images suggesting
twisted or misguided connections, and all in turn serve as images suggestive of the work itself.

Mario Vargas Llosa provides a good treatment of the temporal circularity of the narrative in García Márquez' novel, a
structure in which he says "el episodio se muerde la cola,
comienza y termina en el mismo sitio."[18] He shows that this
circularity is usually achieved through telling an important fact
of the narrative, making a "salto hacia el pasado remoto y rela-
ción lineal de los hechos hasta coincidir con lo mencionado en
la apertura."[19] Vargas Llosa stops short of a complete explanation of the process by not bringing out that many times these
"saltos" in time are achieved without the slightest grammatical
indication of having taken place. For example, on page 60 of the
novel we encounter Melquíades trying to fix the player piano
on the night of a party at the Buendía home: "Melquíades, ya
casi ciego, desmigajándose de decrepitud, recurrió a las artes
de su antiquísima sabiduria para tratar de componerlo. Al fin
José Arcadio Buendía logró mover por equivocación un dis-
positivo atascado, y la música salió." We notice that Melquíades' attempts to fix the instrument, expressed in the
preterite, are immediately followed by other verbs in the preterite, continuing the forward motion of the episode. The narration seems to be linear; there is no indication that any "salto"
has taken place. Things proceed in this manner for several
pages, until Melquíades again becomes the focus of attention in
the narrative:

Cuando la respiración de Melquíades empezó a oler, Arcadio lo
llevó a bañarse al río los jueves en la mañana. Pareció me-
jorar. . . . Así pasó mucho tiempo sin que nadie lo viera en la
casa, salvo la noche en que hizo un conmovedor esfuerzo por
componer la pianola. (Pp. 68–69)

The grammatical structure of the narrative, which has been
one long string of preterite verbs in causal succession, gives no
basis for perceiving a jump in time. The jump connecting the
latter passage with the former is an illegal one; it defies its own
grammatical and causal linearity. This temporal loop, which
occurs many times throughout the novel, is yet another variation of the short circuit or forbidden connection, and as such
mirrors the structure of the novel as we have defined it.

Objects with No Nexus

As we have said, the novel has a short circuit in that its
connection between manuscript, text, and tempest is logically
forbidden. Conversely, the survival of the novel after Macondo's storm makes it an object with no nexus, that is, an
object that ought to be connected to something, but seems not
to be. The novel, by demands of internal evidence, ought to be
connected to the manuscript. But when the winds devour the
latter, the former seems suddenly to emerge as an entity apart
from every logical ground or connection. The unjustified connection and the unjustified disconnection are two sides of a coin
in *Cien años de soledad*'s pattern of ambiguity. Just as the
puzzling linkage is echoed throughout the novel's imagery, so
also is the puzzling absence of linkage. When José Arcadio
Buendía and his party of explorers find the remains of a Spanish
galleon, miles from any water (p. 18); when Úrsula sees a pot of
water boiling on her work table without having been near a fire,
and sees Amaranta's bassinet move about the room of its own
accord (p. 37); and when Aureliano Buendía answers a telephone call in Macondo's North American community, long

since a ghost town (p. 324), each is in a way imitating what
happens to the reader at the end of the novel. The galleon
ought to be contiguous to some body of water, the pot ought to
be next to a fire, and the bassinet next to someone's hand. The
telephone call ought to be temporally connected to the existence of the gringos and their banana empire. However, all are
not. The novel ought to be connected to the existence of the
manuscript, and therefore ought to perish with it. These events
are *ungrounded* in the philosopher's use of the term "ground,"
meaning the cause for a phenomenon or idea. The events exist
in logical solitude. The philosophical concept of ground or
world-ground probably originates from the ground we build
from—a firm, sure starting point. Not only do things in *Cien
años de soledad* leave the ground in the extended philosophical
sense, but they also do so in the concrete sense. The ascension
of Remedios, la Bella, into heaven (p. 205) is an ungrounding in
both senses, because it is a phenomenon with no apparent
cause. Padre Nicanor's levitations, induced by nothing more
than cups of chocolate (p. 77), fall into the same category.

Numerous images in the novel reinforce the concept of a
structure ungrounded or disconnected: the cutting of an um-
bilical cord (pp. 20, 346), the woman in the gypsy carnival
"decapitada todas las noches" (p. 35), Macondo's quarantine
against the plague of insomnia (p. 46), Remedios, la Bella's
immunity to any worldly contagion (p. 172), and Amaranta Úrsula and Aureliano in their trysts, "flotando en un universo
vacío" (p. 342). To be sure, the images harmonize with the
novel's theme of personal solitude. However, at the same time,
all reflect the work itself, which exists in its own form of solitude, "flotando en un universo vacío."

Self-destruction, Self-reconstruction

We have maintained that as a representation of a reality, the
novel deconstructs and reconstructs itself ad infinitum. Earlier

we presented a case for why this is so, based upon the logical reactions of a reader faced with the textual evidence of the novel's ending. We find further corroboration for this view if we consider how often the novel's contents mirror their container, that is, how often the characters and events perform according to the same self-destructive and often self-reconstructive pattern.

The pattern is obvious in the behavior of most members of the Buendía family. José Arcadio Buendía devotes unending, mystical fervor to his alchemy experiments, only to smash his equipment in a sudden fit, and renounce any further inquiry for a sedentary, tree-tied life like that of a family pet (p. 74). Amaranta tortures herself by placing her hand in the fire (p. 100). She greatly desires Colonel Gerineldo Márquez, but rejects his advances (p. 123). One of the bastard sons of Colonel Aureliano Buendía has a special talent for destroying everything he touches (pp. 133, 191). The Colonel himself loses every battle he undertakes, writes love poetry that he later burns, survives incredible danger in war only to try later to take his own life, and wages an idealistic war, later to renounce his ideals in the armistice. The continual doing-undoing pattern of his life is appropriately typified by the craft of making little gold fish, which absorbs his later years: "cambiaba los pescaditos por monedas de oro, y luego convertía las monedas de oro en pescaditos, y así sucesivamente, de modo que tenía que trabajar cada vez más a medida que más vendía, para satisfacer un círculo vicioso exasperante" (p. 173). Later, he ceases selling the fish, so as to concentrate entirely on their effacement and replacement: "Había diecisiete. Desde que decidió no venderlos, seguía fabricando dos pescaditos al día, y cuando completaba veinticinco volvía a fundirlos en el crisol para empezar a hacerlos de nuevo" (p. 227). Amaranta behaves the same way as she knits her own funeral shroud, undoing her mortal existence with each intricate turn; so does Aureliano Segundo, as he devotes great energy to home repairs, and then smashes everything in the household; and so does Amaranta Úrsula in her housework, "resolviendo problemas domésticos que ella misma creaba y haciendo mal ciertas cosas que corregía al día siguiente" (p. 322). Fernanda del Carpio understands the essence of this behavior in Amaranta Úrsula's husband:

> Viéndolo montar picaportes y desconectar relojes, Fernanda se preguntó si no estaría incurriendo también en el vicio de *hacer para deshacer,* como el coronel Aureliano Buendía con los pescaditos de oro, Amaranta con los botones y la mortaja, José Arcadio Segundo con los pergaminos y Úrsula con los recuerdos. (Pp. 267–68; my emphasis)

This pattern in the family's behavior is a reflection of the complex of collapsing, recuperating motifs at the novel's end. Though most characters seem to be engaged in undoing more than redoing, the repetitive nature of their behavior as a group cannot be ignored. Colonel Aureliano Buendía seems to be a paradigm of all the members of the family. His eternal elaboration, effacement, and re-elaboration of the golden fish is suggestive of the behavior of the family in general. Furthermore, these actions reflect the novel, with its eternal undoing. Everything undoes itself, so that even the undoing is undone. The description of the last vestiges of Macondo's past applies equally well to *Cien años de soledad* as a whole: "Era lo último que iba quedando de un pasado cuyo aniquilamiento no se consumaba, porque seguía aniquilándose indefinidamente, consumiéndose dentro de sí mismo, acabándose a cada minuto pero sin acabar de acabarse jamás" (pp. 339–40).

Abrupt Reversals

As we have mentioned, the reader's reaction to the ending of the novel is subject to abrupt reversals. He is led along the path

of a given hypothesis up to a point, at which the force of contradiction makes him suddenly recoil. The reader's function with
respect to the novel seems to have its equivalent within the
work in various sorts of interpersonal transactions, which
though they may not have logical contradictions, feature similarly abrupt reversals. An example: José Arcadio Buendía's
efforts in the alchemy laboratory seem at last to be paying off.
Even the sceptical Úrsula "hasta dio gracias a Dios por la inven-
ción de la alquimia" (p. 32). A crowd shows up to marvel at the
feat, until

> De tanto mostrarlo, [José Arcadio Buendía] terminó frente a su
> hijo mayor, que en los últimos tiempos apenas se asomaba por el
> laboratorio. Puso frente a sus ojos el mazacote seco y
> amarillento, y le preguntó: "¿Qué te parece?" José Arcadio,
> sinceramente, contestó:
> —Mierda de perro. (P. 32)

The same sort of abrupt, even violent change in directions
occurs when Amaranta tells Pietro Crespi, after months of encouraging and even fighting for his attention, that she would
not marry him even if she were dead (p. 98); when Rebeca
suddenly kills José Arcadio, the man "que la había hecho feliz"
(p. 118); and when Colonel Aureliano Buendía's attempted suicide is foiled by the doctor, who instead of marking on the
Colonel's chest the exact location of the heart as requested,
marked "el único punto por donde podía pasar una bala sin
lastimar ningún centro vital" (p. 150). There is a variety of
similar cases, in which someone is attracted in a given direction
and then surprised and turned back. In all instances, the
characters of Macondo are only too willing to be led into these
frustrating reversals. They appear to possess the same "willing
suspension of disbelief" that characterizes the reader. The similarity is not casual, for the characters are definitions of the
reader.

Solipsistic Encounters

Many are the situations in the novel that lead towards a solipsistic outlook. Usually these images involve characters whose perceptions are contradictory, for example: José Arcadio fails after considerable travail to find a route to Riohacha (p. 28), but Úrsula easily finds the route several years later (p. 38). José Arcadio Segundo sees hundreds of strikers killed by machine guns and their bodies hauled off by train into the sea, but no one else seems to have noticed (p. 261). Members of the Buendía family see José Arcadio Segundo in Melquíades' room, but a soldier searching the house sees nothing (p. 265). Aureliano Babilonia stops at a familiar pharmacy, but finds instead a carpenter's shop; the woman answering the door insists that there was never a pharmacy there (p. 347).

Some things seem to have different existences at different moments. Officials capture someone who by every indication appears to be señor Brown, the banana magnate. The next day he appears before the court with dark skin, speaking perfect Spanish (pp. 255–56). Santa Sofía de la Piedad has "la rara virtud de no existir por completo sino en el momento oportuno" (p. 102).

The relativity of perception is suggested repeatedly. The priest's comment to Aureliano the translator, as the latter searches through church records in order to find his ancestry, is a humorous example:

> . . . el párroco artrítico que lo observaba desde la hamaca le preguntó compasivamente cual era su nombre.
> —Aureliano Buendía—dijo el.
> —Entonces no te mates buscando —exclamó el párroco con una convicción terminante—. Hace muchos años hubo aquí una calle que se llamaba así, y por esos entonces la gente tenía la costumbre de ponerles a los hijos los nombres de las calles.
> (P. 344)

These and other images fit into the overall structure of the novel, which at its end is a solipsistic standoff. The validity (existence) of the manuscript may be maintained, but only at the expense of the validity of the storm or novel. In turn, the validity of either storm or text may only be lasting if something else becomes invalid. Because the text, which is directly perceptible to the reader, is involved in the relativistic trade-off, the reader is perhaps prompted to question his own validity, remarking along with the arthritic priest just mentioned: "A mí me bastaría con estar seguro de que tú y yo existimos en este momento" (p. 345).

Cien años de soledad's status as a signifier is ambiguous, involving an equivocal interplay of the published work, Melquíades' manuscript, and the storm. This ambiguity of closure, in the sense of ending, is also an ambiguity of closure in the sense of self-containment or enclosure. By examining some of the predominant motifs of the novel—short circuits, objects with no nexus, self-destruction, and self-restitution, abrupt reversals and solipsistic encounters—we have tried to show that the novel's contents conform to its container. The represented world of Macondo consistently imitates the structure of *Cien años de soledad*. Perhaps we might do better to say that the container imitates the contents, or even, that they imitate each other. In any case, looking at one helps us define the other.

Repetition and Return

This study has touched lightly upon a manifestation of ambiguity that is perhaps the most elementary in life or art. *Cien años de soledad* invites us to consider the matter explicitly. Repetition seems by nature to be ambiguous, its principal features being sameness and difference. Let us consider repetitive items one, two, and three. Item one is the source element. Item two is repetitious for two reasons: because it is the same as item one, and because it is *not* the same as item one. By being sequential to item one, it qualifies as an individual entity, and without that distinction, it would not be repetitive. But without being the same, it could not be repetitive either. Likewise, item three is a repetition of the previous two elements because it is equivalent to them and at the same time different from them. By virtue of its context, each element is unique; by virtue of its quality, each is equivalent to the others.

Repetition is both the affirmation and the negation of sequence. If item two repeats item one, it somehow returns to what is essential to item one, and adheres to that essence. The observer of repetition necessarily returns in his mind to the previous element and dwells upon it. Simultaneously, repetitive elements separate or distinguish themselves. Item two maintains its difference from item one in the very act of reproducing item one, and the observer accompanies by perceiving sequence. Repetition within time seems to lead to contradictory perceptions. On the one hand, one might concentrate on the sameness of repeating elements and tend to regard the phenomenon as infinitely deep and immutable. On the other, one might concentrate on the elements' differences and be led to a perception of time's infinite breadth and transition. In movement through space, the contradictory tension produced by repetition is the same. Objects seem both to move and to be stationary. The line returns upon itself, so that linearity and "punctuality" are simultaneously present.[20]

Cien años de soledad is a showcase of the ambiguity of repetition. The preceding section of this analysis has shown how essential patterns in the novel tend to repeat themselves ad infinitum. While the context makes each motif distinctive, there remains within them a common core. Each member of the Buendía family has individual characteristics, but at the same time the essential qualities of each are the same. Perhaps for this reason it is hard to speak of a protagonist in the novel;

the protagonist would have to be the whole family, because each member is somehow a variation of the other. Emir Rodríguez Monegal refers to this reduplication as the theme underlying the entire novel. Commenting on the obvious repetition of names in various permutations through the several generations, he notes that the repetition

> sirve para fines distintos que los de la mera confusión. Sirve . . . para acentuar la reiteración dentro de la variedad, la simbiosis de identidad personal e identidad familiar que es, en síntesis, el tema profundo del libro. Tantos Aurelianos acaban por confundirse en un solo Aureliano; tantas Rebecas terminan por solaparse en una sola. El individuo se multiplica y se diluye. La estirpe triunfa.[21]

The types of repetition appearing in *Cien años de soledad* (syntactic, thematic, enumerative, etc.) have already received considerable attention.[22] What we wish to emphasize here is that there is more to this repetition than a simple reproduction of like elements in sequence. To begin considering its implications, we may notice the geometric dimension in the imagery having to do with repetition. Ursula's response to the conduct of her family is typical of the tendency of this imagery to be expressed in geometric terms: "'Ya esto me lo sé de memoria,' gritaba Úrsula. 'Es como si el tiempo diera vueltas en redondo y hubiéramos vuelto al principio'" (p. 169). In the novel, the line turns back upon itself and becomes circular. This movement suggests the archetypal "vuelta al principio" or return to the source, where all appears to be profound and immortally stable.[23] Pilar Ternera appears to discover this source through repetition after one hundred years of interaction with the Buendía clan:

> No había ningún misterio en el corazón de un Buendía, que fuera impenetrable para ella, porque un siglo de naipes y de experiencia le había enseñado que la historia de la familia era un

engranaje de repeticiones irreparables, una rueda giratoria.
(P. 334)

There appears to be permanence, even knowledge, at the point
of origin to which the linear progression returns. This is the
pattern we see in the lives of so many characters in the novel.
José Arcadio both intellectually and physically travels outward
in search of discovery, but he winds up at the center point, the
point of profound fixity, tied to a tree in the patio of his home.[24]
Colonel Aureliano Buendía leads numerous military forays
throughout the country, and in the end hardly leaves his small
goldsmith's shop. José Arcadio Segundo crusades for social justice, but finally retires to complete seclusion in Melquíades'
chamber. The geometry of this return is capsulized in the
dream José Arcadio Buendía has before going insane:

> Cuando estaba solo, José Arcadio Buendía se consolaba con el
> sueño de los cuartos infinitos. Soñaba que se levantaba de la
> cama, abría la puerta y pasaba a otro cuarto igual, con la misma
> cama de cabecera de hierro forjado, el mismo sillón de mimbre
> y el mismo cuadrito de la Virgen de los Remedios en la pared
> del fondo. De ese cuarto pasaba a otro exactamente igual, . . . y
> luego a otro exactamente igual, hasta el infinito. Le gustaba irse
> de cuarto en cuarto, como en una galería de espejos paralelos,
> hasta que Prudencio Aguilar le tocaba el hombro. Entonces
> regresaba de cuarto en cuarto, despertando hacia atrás, recor-
> riendo el camino inverso, y encontraba a Prudencio Aguilar en
> el cuarto de la realidad. (P. 124)

Sequence and return are the essence of this passage. Through
the medium of repetition, José Arcadio goes forward without
going anywhere, for each forward motion has its corresponding
return. José Arcadio Buendía, perhaps more than any other
character, suggests in the pattern of his life the line's return
upon itself. Once this return is completed, linear time ceases
for him to move forward. José Arcadio remarks: "sigue siendo

lunes, como ayer. Mira el cielo, mira las paredes, mira las begonias. También hoy es lunes" (p. 73).

In numerous dimensions, the novel is return and repetition. This does not mean, however, that it simply conforms to a circular pattern. Like the ambiguity of repetition itself, it insists on simultaneously being both circular (or pointlike) and linear. If we consider the novel's images of repetition and return without paying attention to numerous images in exact contradiction, we are only seeing half the picture. The images of immutability we have mentioned are counterbalanced by utterly transitory, sequential, and linear images. The passage concerning Pilar Ternera's conclusions about the essentially repetitive nature of the Buendía family, which we mentioned earlier as an example of constancy through repetition, has a final line which produces the opposite impression: "la historia de la familia era un engranaje de repeticiones irreparables, una rueda giratoria *que hubiera seguido dando vueltas hasta la eternidad, de no haber sido por el desgaste progresivo e irremediable del eje*" (p. 334; my emphasis).

Wearing away, irremediable progression. An eternal ticket for a train that never stops traveling (p. 339), a palm whose life line is chopped off at the base of the thumb by the anchor of death (p. 101), manuscripts whose contents are irrepeatable since time immemorial and for ever more (p. 351), and a race condemned to one hundred years of solitude, without a second opportunity upon the earth (p. 351)—these are images of linearity, bound to the passage of time, in which all is irreversible. Images of infinite similitude are counterbalanced by those of absolute uniqueness and originality: "nadie pudo concebir un motivo para que Rebeca asesinara al hombre que la había hecho feliz. Ese fue tal vez el único misterio que nunca se esclareció en Macondo" (pp. 117–18); "Fue el primer entierro y el más concurrido que se vió en el pueblo" (p. 69); "era el único en un siglo que había sido engendrado con amor" (p. 346). José Ar-

cadio Buendía's dream of infinite repetition has its converse in a
dream by Colonel Aureliano: "Soñó que entraba en una casa
vacía, de paredes blancas, y que lo inquietaba la pesadumbre
de ser el primer ser humano que entraba en ella" (p. 227).
Uniqueness versus sameness, linearity versus pointedness,
transition versus stability—each of these either/or propositions
becomes undecidable in *Cien años de soledad.*

The ambiguity between linearity and its opposite brings us
back to the ambiguity of tempest, text, and manuscript analyzed earlier. Like the analogous drawing (fig. 4.1) the situation
represents a crisis of linearity and nonlinearity. The storm bestows an irreversability on the narrative. That absolutely sequential quality is not unusual to our perception of the world of
action. But it makes *everything* irrepeatable, including the
written word. We normally consider the written word to be
timeless, immortal, and infinitely repeatable; but here it is
supposed to be irrepeatable. The existence of the text contra-
dicts that irrepeatability, and somehow makes the word and the
actions seem transitory, and yet transcendent.

The Problem of Tone

The line sets its perceiver in motion and leads him along a
given course. That part of us centered in "the lower reaches of
the soul," which is prone to predict meaning, seems more than
willing to follow a line to its end, and perhaps even beyond its
end. The line, therefore, is often a dangerous form; many colloquial expressions point out the upsetting evil that lurks at the
end of the line. To "get a person into (or on) a line," for example,
means to engage him in conversation so that a confederate can
rob him. The idea of deception is often associated with a line, as
in the expressions "he tried to feed me a line," its analogue
"they've been stringing me along," and perhaps even "he swallowed that lie hook, line and sinker." The line seems to be the

perfect image to describe the process of engaging a person's projective, predictive capacity in order to lead him into a trap.

There is a type of humor that thrives on this very reaction. In *Jokes and Their Relation to the Unconscious* Sigmund Freud gives a classic example, that of making someone look ridiculous by yelling "Catch!" and throwing him a ball tied to a string so that it jerks to a halt before reaching him.[25]

We have seen that the pattern of abrupt reversal is found frequently in *Cien años de soledad.* There is essentially no difference between this pattern and that of the string-tied ball trick. A linear dimension, with a sudden ending, is clear in both cases. The recurring pattern of abrupt reversal appears to be exemplary of the novel as a whole, with its suddenly contradictory ending. The question we must now ask is this: to what extent is the novel itself a sort of expectation joke, in which we as readers are encouraged to swallow a narrative line? If the novel defines itself, as we have postulated, and if the novel jokes with the reader, we should expect to be able to find joking and jokes discussed within the novel. Indeed, this turns out to be the case. We have maintained that various interpersonal transactions suggest the relationship between reader and text. As an example, we cited the relationship between Remedios, la Bella, and her several suitors, who are strongly drawn towards her, but constantly turned away and frustrated by her "corazón indecifrable" (p. 142). In this interaction, there is the suggestion of a joke, "una trampa diabólica en el centro de la candidez" (p. 172). To the extent that Remedios is equivalent to a text and her suitors to readers, the joke is a cruel one on both suitors and readers. But is it a joke at all? Through it all, her face is the picture of innocence. And is not the novel's narrative face the same?

Joking is also associated with Aureliano Babilonia, the last of the Buendía line. This time, however, the literary dimension of the "burla" is more explicit: "No se le había ocurrido hasta entonces que la literatura fuera el mejor juguete que se había inventado para burlarse de la gente" (p. 327). Aureliano learns that literature is a tool for joking. But does he use it for such? Serious and reserved, Aureliano "no era hombre de burlas" (p. 306), at least that is what Fernanda decides. Aureliano's friends cannot decide amongst themselves whether or not he is tricking them: Aureliano "estaba más cerca de Gabriel que de los otros [amigos]. El vínculo nació la noche en que él habló del coronel Aureliano Buendía, y Gabriel fue el único que no creyó que se estuviera burlando de alguien" (p. 329). Aureliano is a perfect example of the straight-faced might-be joker. We cannot decide just how to read him. Once again, we have a case where a character reflects the novel; Aureliano's posture and the novel's posture as possible tricksters are the same.

A final example of the joke motif in the novel should suffice to show the possibility that *Cien años de soledad's* tone is that of a dubious "burlador." The relationship between audience and work(s) of art in the following passage about a movie theater appears paradigmatic of the relationship between the reader and the novel. The people of Macondo

> Se indignaron con las imágenes vivas que el próspero comerciante don Bruno Crespi proyectaba en el teatro con taquillas de bocas de león, porque un personaje muerto y sepultado en una película, y por cuya desgracia se derramaron lágrimas de aflicción, reapareció vivo y convertido en árabe en la película siguiente. El público que pagaba dos centavos para compartir las vicisitudes de los personajes, no pudo soportar aquella burla inaudita y rompió la silletería. El alcalde, a instancias de don Bruno Crespi, explicó mediante un bando, que el cine era una máquina de ilusión que no merecía los desbordamientos pasionales del público. (P. 194)

Humorous is the exaggerated gullibility of the audience, which considers the reemergence of someone who is supposed to have died a "burla inaudita." This audience's reaction, however, is not so different from the situation we find ourselves in as we come to the end of *Cien años de soledad*. The episode in relation to the novel as a whole reminds us of Chinese boxes, the contents replicating their container. In both the novel and this episode, the issue is the irretrievability of events in time. The movie hero's death and Macondo's disappearance with the storm are analogous, because both are irreversible in the linear, historical perspective. Following the historical line leads us to modern philosophies such as existentialism, wherein individuals' existence is seen as fleeting and nontranscendent, where their ties with past and future are limited, and where uniqueness is perceived as alienation. This is the line of solitude; we are moved to follow such a line in the novel, with "lágrimas de aflicción." But at the end of the line lies a surprise. The dead movie hero reappears. Likewise, the manuscript, by all rights nonexistent, reappears in the form of the novel. Suddenly it seems as if the line we have so faithfully followed is a line we have swallowed![26]

Cien años de soledad therefore has an ambiguity of tone that makes the reader uncertain about how to "take" the novel. As we noted earlier, the reader enters into a willing contract with his text. In effect, he pays his "dos centavos para compartir las vicisitudes de los personajes," he invests something in good faith to receive some sort of fictional truth to which he can respond. His contribution is the willingness to suspend his disbelief and be led where the text will take him. *Cien años de soledad*, with its fantastic and exaggerated elements, teaches the reader quickly to set aside his incredulity, and he willingly does so because, in spite of its exaggeration, the novel seems to portray a real world in its abstract or spiritual dimension. It portrays the story of Latin America, with its feudalistic society, civil wars, banana republics, its faith, idealism, and dealings with death.[27] In addition, the novel seems to display an internal validity by keeping its promises. For example, it does not

foreshadow a pig's tail without delivering a pig's tail. The obliteration of Macondo has the ring of artistic truth; according to
Barbara Herrnstein Smith's criteria, it has the makings of a
strong, artistically valid ending. Nothing better spells finality.
However, obliteration is itself obliterated, because of the ultimate "literation" of the novel's survival. The novel seems suddenly to jump into view, alive and well, like the "personaje
muerto" in the passage. And how should we react as readers?
On the one hand, we are encouraged, like the moviegoers, to
see the whole matter as a "burla inaudita," an artistic "trampa
diabólica" in which we are the victim. All that has seemed valid
historically, philosophically, or artistically now seems to lose its
truth when we respond this way.[28]

We may perhaps soothe our cheated egos if we detach ourselves from the work by maintaining that the novel, like the
movie in the passage is but a "máquina de ilusión que no
merece los desbordamientos pasionales del público." But this
response, often called artistic distancing, might also be called
unartistic distancing, because it is a repudiation of the very
responses that are essential to much of the artistic experience.

Invalidity and illusion: are these our only choices? There
seems to be another: that the novel is valid, artistically and
otherwise, because even in its ultimate "trampa" it is keeping a
promise and fulfilling a prophecy. *Cien años de soledad* is a
mirrored novel. As the analysis of motifs such as short circuits,
abrupt reversals, self-destruction, and self-replacement has
shown, the novel's contents mirror its container. The work's
final undoing has in this sense been visible from the beginning;
therefore, the final undoing is at the same time a knot tying
everything together. The reader's predicament is what faces the
reader in any case of ambiguity—true or false; this or that?
While usually the ambiguity is centered in plot, structures, or
competing levels, here the enigma affects the validity of the
work as a whole. In the end, we are faced with an impossible

situation. Because the work unabashedly destroys its logical consistency at the end, it marks itself as untrue. However, it has prepared and prefigured the ending since its inception. The inconsistent is consistent. The response in such a case will be an eternal surprise, a "delirio hermenéutico" and "un permanente vaivén entre el alborozo y el desencanto."

5

Transverse and Universe in
Grande sertão: veredas

Some of the most prominent words in João Guimarães Rosa's novel, *Grande sertão: veredas*,[1] point in opposing directions. "Nonada," the first word of the work, is obviously related to the word "nada"—nothing. By saying "nothing," however, the word says "something." "Nonada" refers to something, something of little value or consequence, a "ninharia," but nevertheless and most assuredly something. The word's composition, with the archaic "non" ("não") plus "nada," suggests this contradictory situation. On the one hand, "non" seems to duplicate and emphasize the sense of "nada," but on the other, "non" might act as a negating element, as in "não-intervenção" and "não-conformista." "Nonada," by being "non-nothing," becomes something.

The last word of the novel, like the first, is prominently detached from a sentence. "Travessia" denotes first of all the act of crossing a region, continent or sea, of going from one end of something to the other. It also refers to a long, open road. But this notion of movement in a single direction is undermined when one considers the word's etymology, and its etymological relatives. The Latin roots "versus" or "vertere" involve the notion of turning. "Transvert," a word springing from the same roots, means among other things "to reverse." "Transversal" means "lying across" and in geometry refers to the intersection of lines. In Portuguese, "travessia" may refer in nautical terminology to a crosswind or to a zigzag course. So the notion of a single line or of movement in a single direction is contradicted by that of intersecting lines and movement in opposing directions.

"Veredas," a word similarly detached in the work's title, is polysemic also. On the one hand, "veredas" refers to narrow paths upon the ground. On the other, in Minas Gerais (the setting of the novel) it may refer to small streams of water surrounded by *buriti* palms. In both cases small, dividing courses are involved, but where the substance of one is earth, the substance of the other is water. In the novel, both types of courses are called "veredas," and occasionally it seems unclear which is which (see, for example, pp. 59, 76, 303, 363, and 432). As if to strike a compromise, "vereda" offers still another definition; it may be a swamp. The plural form of the word and even the *V* in its visual aspect[2] suggest the diverging paths, directions, or meanings of the word itself.

In effect, each of these words intersects itself. I will suggest in this chapter that the same sort of ambiguous crossing or "travessia" is essential to the novel on several levels. It is a very contagious concept, infecting most of the recurring images in the work—the bifurcating "veredas," the "encruzilhada" and "redemunho" ("redemoinho"), which is the product of opposing currents of air. The crossing itself seems to be a symbol of the disjunction (V) that is central to the concept of ambiguity. We will see, however, that this disjunction is so prevalent that it becomes a unifying element in the work. Division integrates; the intersection of opposing currents somehow moves in a single direction. The tranverse (movement from one state to another) and the universe (movement towards oneness) coexist.

Transparent and Opaque Language

Some time ago, I saw a clever sideshow in one of the traveling carnivals in Brazil's Northeast, entitled "A mulher-gorila." For two cruzeiros, the show offered spectators the chance to see a girl become transformed before their eyes into a grunting ape. With a little "suspension of disbelief" on my part (the ape costume was not completely convincing), I found the performance quite astounding. The girl, dancing gently to accordion music, really *did* seem to fade away and become a gorilla. And in a moment, the gorilla would dissolve and become the girl, and so on for a few more metamorphoses until the show would be over.

The illusion of a human being changing into a gorilla was accomplished by means of selective lighting and a semi-transparent veil. The gorilla was located directly behind the girl, the veil separating one from the other. When the girl was entirely visible, strong lighting was upon both her and the veil. Under these circumstances the veil was entirely opaque. Gradually, the lighting on the girl and the veil diminished, while at the same time light was increasingly cast upon the gorilla behind. A lighted background behind the gorilla, the same color as the lighted veil, made it appear as if the veil maintained its opacity, when actually it was becoming transparent as the front lighting decreased. There was a moment of confusion, when the silhouette of the girl was superimposed upon the dark figure of the gorilla. When the girl slipped away in complete darkness, the image presented to the eye was totally that of a gorilla.

The ambiguous veil, or scrim, was an essential device in the illusion, for by means of lights it transformed itself from a visible backdrop to an essentially invisible medium, appearing to remain a backdrop all the while.

This same veil, sometimes transparent and sometimes opaque, will serve as my model for this discussion of João Guimarães Rosa's novel, *Grande sertão: veredas*. The work's language is analogous to the veil, in that it appears to waver between the status of a transparent, representational medium, and that of an opaque object that obscures any representation that might lie behind it.

Writers have generally found it difficult to discuss Guimarães Rosa without becoming involved in his peculiar use of language. This analysis of *Grande sertão: veredas* will be no ex-

ception. Many inquiries into the author's language have been of
the microscopic sort, classifying his transformations of standard
Portuguese prose, and subjecting them to close scrutiny in
passages more or less out of context.[3] Here I propose a more
macroscopic approach to the matter. Rather than emphasizing
the different categories of linguistic peculiarities, I will emphasize their similar artistic effects. Considering these effects, I
intend to examine how the unique linguistic character of the
novel contributes to its overall significance, and how it functions not as a mere embellishment, but as an integral factor in
the work's meaning.

Narrative is concerned with the representation of characters
and actions in the form of a story. The term "representation" is
significant, for it suggests making something present again, as
if the content of a particular story has a reality of its own, which
is somehow recreated or brought back into presence through
language. The story is able to become "present" to the mind of
the reader or listener to the extent that the medium of expression itself is *not* present. The more transparent the discourse,
that is, the more the discourse acts as a medium for conveying
something else, the more vivid the representation.

Going back to the veil analogy, we may say that the story is
behind or underlies the expression in the same way that the
figure (gorilla) is behind the veil. Actual experience may be
immediate, that is, unmediated. But a story, which is con-
ventionally the reconstruction of past experience, is necessarily medium bound. This being the case, there is actually a
more intimate connection between the representation and the
medium than the veil analogy would suggest. Perhaps a pho-
tographic negative or a motion picture film is more fitting as an
analogy in this respect. Just as there can be no image without
the transparency, there can be no story without the mediating
veil of language.

But what happens when the representing medium begins to
lose its transparency? Like some worn-out movie print, full of

scratches, spots or dust specks, it might begin to call attention to itself enough to distract from the representation. Like a veil whose texture is appropriately illuminated, it might become so conspicuous as to hide the object behind it.

The language of *Grande sertão: veredas* presents both of these mutually exclusive properties by telling a story, and yet creating a strong potential for obscuring the same. It is a veil that both hides and reveals. The reader is apt to be faced with a disjunction at every turn: representation, or nonrepresentation? He must decide between the two, but whatever the decision, it is apt to be provisory and dubious. Riobaldo, the work's narrator, remarks frequently that "Viver é negócio muito perigoso." We shall see that in the novel living and reading are about the same. "Ler é perigoso" may be considered an appropriate refrain to describe the reader's response to the novel's ambiguity.

Unlike many modern novels, *Grande sertão: veredas'* obscurity is not the product of plotlessness. On the contrary, the novel has a story full of action, conflict, and enigma—a narrative structure complete and satisfying in its own right. As Jon S. Vincent has said, *Grande sertão: veredas* "is, for a multivalent work, extraordinarily controlled. Though it lacks the facile linearity of the realistic novel . . . it might be taken as an only somewhat jumbled plot, in fact, a cowboy story."[4]

The novel's narrative content demands the attention of the reader, first of all, by right of convention. By tradition, novels are stories, if nothing else. But as we can see, there is intrinsic interest in the story as well. There are enigmas to be solved: What is happening between Riobaldo and Diadorim? Has Riobaldo made a pact with the devil? And there are conflicts to be resolved, such as the war between Riobaldo's band of *jagunços* and that of Hermógenes. The novel contains interesting local color, concerning plants and animals, the social milieu, and the manners of the people. It invites psychological analysis of characters, and comparison with medieval novels of chivalry and the epic. The nonlinear structure of the narrative further draws the attention of the reader, because the story must be pieced together like a puzzle for its chronological dimension to be understood. In short, there are several reasons to substantiate what hardly needs substantiation: that *Grande sertão: veredas* is above all a narrative representation, and that the narration demands the reader's attention in its own right.

Traditionally the language of narration has sought to be inconspicuous. Although actions within the narrative often conform to repetitive patterns, the language itself tries to avoid such patterns. Even when the narrative is in verse, as is the case with epic poetry and many other conventional narrative forms, the repetition of sounds and forms is not likely to be as prevalent as in lyric poetry. In spite of the many examples of narrative in verse, narrative displays an affinity towards prose. We will go into theoretical considerations later, but for now we will simply say that narrative emphasizes what is signified over the signifier itself, and that prose likewise gives relative preeminence to the signified. With prose, expression aspires to be a transparent medium.

However, Guimarães Rosa's novel is far from standard prose. Its expression tends to a great degree towards the norms of poetry. Ralph Freedman, author of a work on the lyrical novel, points out how a narrative work which leans towards lyrical poetry is in a crosscurrent with itself:

> The concept of the lyrical novel is a paradox. Novels are usually associated with storytelling; the reader looks for characters with whom he can identify, for actions in which he may become engaged, or for ideas and moral choices he may see dramatized. Lyrical poetry, on the other hand, suggests the expression of feelings or themes in musical or pictorial patterns. Combining features of both, the lyrical novel shifts the reader's attention from men and events to a formal design.[5]

Grande sertão: veredas shifts the reader's attention toward formal design, but because of the constant underlying presence of its narration, it does so equivocally. Occasionally the very medium that discloses to us the narration also hides the narration, shifting our attention from the signified to the signifier.

Critics generally acknowledge the conspicuous nature of the novel's language. Several have mentioned the book's stylistic obscurity.[6] Paulo Rónai's school edition of selections from Guimarães Rosa suggests how difficult the reading is even for Brazilians. For example, accompanying a four-page selection narrating Riobaldo's meeting with Zé Bebelo, he gives thirty-three notes explaining the meaning of expressions.[7] If a reader actually needs that many explanations, he is apt to lose touch with the representation behind the expression at numerous points.

As already noted, a tendency among analysts of the novel and other works by Guimarães Rosa has been to become intensely involved in linguistic studies, that is, studies based on microscopic problems such as morphology, syntax, vocabulary, and punctuation, to the exclusion of more general semantic considerations. Closely allied to this type of study are those that take into account the numerous rhetorical and poetic devices employed.[8] Once again, these studies generally stress form over content. It might be said that this is the tendency of current criticism, but there is more to it than this in the case of *Grande sertão: veredas*. The novel *asks* to be studied in this matter. One simply does not find such an obsession with style in studies of Jorge Amado, Érico Verissimo, or even Machado de Assis. A tendency of several critics with respect to a given work may not be so different from a tendency in the response of a single reader. The propensity of scholars to analyze devices, vocabulary, and morphological and syntactic transformations suggests that there is a textual factor in the work that encourages the reader to perceive words, sounds or forms out of context, to become involved with the novel's linguistic texture at the expense of its underlying representation.

One way of substantiating this claim is by examining several passages in detail, and postulating reasonable readings. It appears that principles of repetition and fragmentation are at work in most of these passages. Repetition has the effect of thrusting certain elements of the stream of language into the foreground of our attention, by inviting, perhaps even impelling the mind to perform a primitive analysis of comparison and contrast. The tendency of this analysis is to focus on fragments of language rather than on larger, more meaningful composite structures. Following are some of the more representative devices:[9]

(1) Neologisms. A frequent device in the novel, neologisms usually involve a transformation of existing words, and in this sense are repetitions of the old, with something new incorporated: "O senhor viu onça . . . *raivável,* pelos filhos?" (p. 123); "Sobrestive um momento, fechados os olhos, *sufruía* aquilo, com outras minhas forças" (p. 221); and "Lugar meu tinha de ser a *concruz* dos caminhos" (p. 317). These words seem to prompt an analysis in which we compare the coined word with existing words: "raivável" with "raiva," "sufruía" with "sofrer" and "fruir," and "concruz" with "cruz." On the basis of these cores of sameness, fragments that are different from the original words beg for our perception: "–ável," /su/ instead of /so/, and "con." We perceive at this point isolated morphemes, and in one case phonemes. That is, we tend to examine language with a magnifying glass, and to perceive its texture. One possibility with neologisms is that the reader simply will not understand their meaning. Several words with foreign roots, such as the English-based "lordeza" (p. 95), are especially susceptible. In these cases, all the reader can possibly perceive is sound (or spelling) instead of sense.

(2) Peculiarities in Orthography. One common practice in the novel is the unnecessary use of accent marks, even by the standards of the old orthography: "Berimbáu" (p. 183); and "Bebél" (p. 183). The redundant use of both dashes and quotation marks is standard: "Ateado no que pensei, eu sem querer disse alto:—'. . .Só o demo. . .' E:—'Uém?...'—um deles, espantado, me indagou. Aí, teimei e interei: —'Só o Que-Não-Fala, o Que-Não-Ri, o Muito-Sério—o cão extremo!'" (p. 308). One possible effect of these practices is to direct the readers' attention to writing *as writing*, and consequently to distract from what is signified.

The passage just cited displays another salient feature of the novel's punctuation—the abundant use of ellipses. This device produces the impression of fragmentation, and a syntactical looseness. The use of periods to set off single words or small sentence fragments is another common stylistic device, which appears to have the same effect: "—Nonada. Tiros que o senhor ouviu foram de briga de homem, não, Deus esteja" (p. 9); "Conto o que fui e vi, no levantar do dia. Auroras." (p. 460); and "Existe é homem humano. Travessia" (p. 460). With this sort of asyndetic language, fragments begin to assume preeminence over their connective system.

(3) Pleonasm. Redundancies abound in the work's verbal structure: "comer, beber, apreciar mulher, brigar e o *fim final*" (p. 45); and "recebi dela uma carta . . . escrita . . . por *outra alheia* mão" (p. 78). Surely one could say that this device imitates colloquial language. But an additional effect seems once again to place fragments into the foreground. After all elements have been syntactically and logically connected, there is something left over. The redundant elements emerge from the referential system by virtue of being unnecessary.

(4) Reduplicatives. Repeated words are frequent. However, they are often repeated in permutation: "Zé Bebelo gritou: — 'Safa, Safas! . . .'" (p. 458); "a gente ao redor é *duro dura*"

(p. 20); and "Aqui a estória se acabou. Aqui, a estória acabada. Aqui a estória acaba" (p. 454). This repetition with variation seems to urge perception of highlighted words or radical elements when we perceive sameness, and of smaller particles when we perceive difference. Again, fragments emerge out of their meaningful context.

(5) Alliteration. Surely one of the most prevalent features of Guimarães Rosa's style, alliteration seems particularly capable of working against referential communication: "mas mesmo assim sofrendo muitas mortes, e sem meios para descontar essas" (p. 253); "Mas tinha esquecido que estava era enconstado em Zé Bebelo" (p. 253); and "e ficou formado um decreto de pedra pensada: que na hora de os soldados sobrechegarem, eu parava perto de Zé Bebelo; e que ele fizesse feição de trair, eu abocava nele o rifle, efetuava" (p. 253). The dense repetition of /m/ in the first example, the vocalic alliteration involving /ɛ/ and /e/ in the second example, and the pairs of alliteration in /f/, /p/, and /s/ in the third all seem to emphasize signifier at the expense of signified. If we notice alliteration at all, we give attention to phonemes, which in themselves signify nothing. It seems that when sounds, separated from their morphemic contexts, emerge into the foreground of our attention, we begin (even when reading silently) to hear a kind of music, apart from the referential message.[10]

(6) Internal Sound Play. Although repetition of sounds at the beginning of words is probably more obtrusive, there are numerous internal sound plays that create an effect similar to that of alliteration. The first example in number five, for instance, has a dense repetition of /s/ and /z/. Other examples follow. "Eu apertei o pé na alpercata" (p. 253) involves repetition of /per/ in "apertei" and "alpercata," and near-repetition of /pɛ/ in "pé." The sequence "a-cú acôo de acuado" (p. 253) takes sound repetition far beyond simple alliteration. Assonance appears with considerable frequency: "cachoeira, que *cantava pancada*"

(p. 253); "labaredas muito *altas! ah, dava.* O senhor *acha* que menos acho?" (p. 253); and "eu parava *perto* de Zé Bebelo"(p. 253). Here again phonemes, with no semantic component, seem to demand our attention.

Grande sertão: veredas seems remarkable for the density of its alliteration and similar sound play. Surely a certain amount of sound recurrence occurs randomly in any prose. A statistical analysis might be able to prove the uncommon density of sound play in the novel; however, it seems too apparent to require that kind of substantiation. For my part, I will simply suggest the density of these figures of sound by noting that all of the examples in numbers five and six (a mere sampling of occurrences) are taken from a single page, selected more or less at random.

(7) Rhyme. Although not so frequent as assonance or alliteration, rhymes are still sprinkled through the novel: "pão ou pães, é questão de opiniães" (p. 9); "De ouvir, dividi o riso do siso" (p. 198); and "de mim, vim com Diadorim" (p. 231). Once again, as we weigh similarity and difference, we perceive phonemes by themselves as discrete elements. The physical properties of the signifier become conspicuous.

(8) Rhythm Patterns. Word stress, like phonetic quality, is not referential per se. It also may be made conspicuous through repetition: "eles dizem, fim do rumo, terras altas" (p. 9); "Então? Que-Diga? Doideira" (p. 10); "tantos vi, que aprendi. Rincha-Mãe, Sangue-d'Outro, o Muitos-Beiços, o Rasga-em-Baixo, Faca-Fria, o Fancho-Bode, um Treciziano, o Azinhavre" (p. 11); and "E nos usos, nas plantas, nas águas, na terra, no vento . . . Estrumes" (p. 11).

With all the devices discussed above, the force of redundancy or repetition demands that attention be given to individual components rather than inclusive, functional structures. The microstructure emerges out of the macrostructure. Where there was a sentence, there are now words; where there was a

word, there are now morphemes; where there were morphemes, there are now phonemes. The garment becomes a
network of threads; the forest becomes so many trees.[11]

Axes and Crosscurrents

Critics have maintained that poetic devices leave the referential capacity of the novel's language unhindered.[12] This attitude has its convincing points, particularly in many cases of
neologism, onomatopoeia, and rhythmic language accompanying rhythmic action. But it is probably not so convincing in
other cases. While on occasion, form and content coincide, in
other cases they seem to be at odds. In answer to those who
have claimed that the language's poetic tendency supports its
capacity to communicate referential material, and in support of
our contradictory hypothesis, we will briefly look at a couple of
contemporary theories of poetic language. In *Estructura del
lenguaje poético*, Jean Cohen maintains that prose, which he
defines as language geared towards clarity of referential communication, tends toward parallelism of sound and sense. For
example, pauses in speech are appropriately placed after the
expression of complete ideas. Repeating sounds accompany
repeating concepts. According to Cohen, verse is defined in
purely negative terms as what prose is not, that is, as non-
parallelism between sound and sense:

> Con la redundancia [de sonido con sentido] el lenguaje trata de
> construir estructuras fuertes. Es este uno de los principios fun-
> damentales de la estrategia lingüística. Y precisamente este
> principio lo toma la versificación a contrapelo. Parece como si el
> poeta buscase en todo la forma de debilitar las estructuras del
> discurso, como si su objeto, en definitiva, fuese poner di-
> ficultades al mensaje. Esta conclusión es evidentemente para-
> dójica: el verso, considerado tradicionalmente como algo de
> más, nosotros lo reducimos (tal es nuestra opinión) a algo de
> menos. Nos parece una pura negatividad.[13]

The discourse in *Grande sertão: veredas* tends towards what Cohen would call verse, for it features recurrence in sound, *in opposition to* differences in sense:

> El verso no es simplemente distinto de la prosa. Se opone a ella: no es no prosa, sino antiprosa. El discurso en prosa expresa el pensamiento, asimismo "discursivo", lo cual quiere decir que va de idea en idea. Descartes comparaba el pensamiento con una cadena, comparación ésta exacta, pero con una reserva: los eslabones de una cadena son idénticos, mientras que los elementos del pensamiento—y de la palabra que lo expresa—son todos diferentes. Un discurso que repitiese las mismas palabras o las mismas frases no sería un discurso, sino un fracaso de la palabra.
>
> Igual que la prosa, la poesía compone un discurso, es decir que reúne series de términos fonéticamente diferentes. *Pero el verso aplica toda una serie de semejanzas fónicas a la línea de las diferencias semánticas, y es verso en tanto en cuanto que tal hace*.[14]

Cohen illustrates the relationship between sound and sense in poetry and prose with these models:[15]

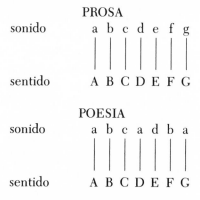

Prose, in other words, tends to make differences in sound parallel differences in sense, while in poetry the tendency is the opposite: "La versificación une los segmentos que separa la

prosa e identifica los términos que la prosa distingue. Procedimientos negativos, pues, que tienden a debilitar la estructuración del mensaje."[16]

One of the principal ambiguities in *Grande sertão: veredas* is
that a narrative work, which qualifies as prose in its outward
appearance and in its referential function, can perhaps be described as well by a definition of poetry as by one of prose. The
novel communicates its narrative message, but at the same
time features the aforementioned "procedimientos negativos . . . que tienden a debilitar la estructuración del mensaje."

Roman Jakobson's theory is another that helps show how
language like that in the novel can work against representation.
It is interesting that his theories introduce the concept of opposing tendencies in language in terms of intersecting axes, a
figure harmonious with the "crossing" that occurs frequently in
the novel's imagery. In his well-known essay, "Linguistics and
Poetics" (1960), Jakobson identifies the message as the central
component in a communicative system, which also includes
the addresser, the addressee, the context, the contact (physical
medium of communication), and the code.[17] Language, he
says, may have different functions, depending on which of
these components the message is focused upon. When the
message concentrates upon the context, it has a *referential*
function. That is, it refers to, describes, or represents the world
in which it is situated. Jakobson describes the *poetic* function as
one in which the message focuses upon itself.[18] According to
these definitions, we have a theoretical invitation to compare
the language of the novel to a veil that is alternately opaque and
transparent. When language assumes the poetic function, the
message focuses upon itself, and when the message is the primary object in view, language in effect becomes opaque. When
language is engaged in the referential function, the message
focuses upon its context, and under these circumstances we
look through the message at something else.

By convention, fictional narratives assume a simulated referential function. They refer to an imaginary context as if it were real. Although that context was never really present, they represent it as if it had been. Surely *Grande sertão: veredas* operates according to this function. But according to Jakobson's discussion of the poetic function, we see that it seems to perform that function as well.

Jakobson says, "No doubt, verse is primarily a recurrent 'figure of sound.'"[19] Recurrence implies equivalence among repeated elements, and the principle of equivalence, whether involving sounds, pauses, or semantics, is essential to poetic language under Jakobson's definition. All language, poetic or not, is a sequence of elements. Poetry's specific difference is that equivalence, which is usually only a matter of *selection* (choice between synonyms, for example) and which usually comes into play only before an expression is produced, becomes a matter of *combination* (connection of elements to produce discourse) and is actually incorporated into the expressed sequence: "*The poetic function projects the principle of equivalence from the axis of selection into the axis of combination.* Equivalence is promoted to the constitutive device of the sequence."[20]

Guimarães Rosa's novel has a language permeated with "recurrent figures of sound." It is a good illustration of how the "principle of equivalence" may be projected from the "axis of selection" into the "axis of combination." By virtue of this poetic function, the message, though referential by definition and convention, seems to turn away from the referent and towards itself.

This discussion of Jakobson and Cohen has tended to be more dichotomous than the theories themselves might justify. Both authors admit that such concepts as prose and poetry, poetic function and referential function are more tendencies towards poles than absolute categories, and both allow for hybridization in any given expression.[21] *Grande sertão: vere-*

das itself attests to the relative status of poetry and prose. If we have emphasized dichotomies here, it has been to call attention to mutually exclusive currents that may act within language.

Discourse may be a means to some other end, or it may be an end in itself. From the standpoint of the reader, a novel's language may be an object of analysis or it may be a medium for analyzing something else. One looks *at* a window to clean it, and he sees its surface, with its dust or streaks, but does not pay attention to the scene outside. On the other hand, one looks outside *through* a window, and he may have a sense of seeing through the window with difficulty, but if he sees what is outside, he does not at the same time focus on the marks on the window's surface. Similarly, a reader may waver between these two modes of perception—looking *through* the medium of language or looking *at* language itself, but it seems he may not adequately perceive both at the same time.[22] Because of the coexistence of impelling narrative content and dense poetic texture, *Grande sertão: veredas* encourages an ambivalent wavering between the two modes.

The Disjunction in "Travessia"

The ambiguity just discussed is portable. Unlike that in *Dom Casmurro*, for example, it features no central enigma in the story around which mutually exclusive motifs revolve. The alternative hypotheses do not take turns presenting themselves through a series of textual motifs (a b a b a b); a series of doubly directed clues (a/b a/b a/b) might come closer to describing the ambiguity, but the description still falls short. Instead, it might be said that there is a single exclusive disjunction, one large A/B, that extends the length of the entire work and which accompanies the reader as he progresses through the work. The novel's story is always present, while at the same time the demands of conspicuous style are practically always present. The language surely fluctuates towards and away from standard prose. But the "wavelength" of this fluctuation is so short, and the density of poetic devices so great that conspicuous language makes its demands nearly constantly. It is as if we were at a fork in the road, and just after choosing one path or the other we were faced with another fork, and then after choosing a path we were faced immediately with another fork, and so on until the end. Reading is dangerous! "Veredas" are everywhere, pointing always in opposing directions. Reading is a passage or crossing of the novel's domain—a "travessia," to use the term from the novel. And the disjunction accompanies the reader at every turn.

The disjunction's movement as just described is along what Jakobson calls the *axis of combination*. Disjunction accompanies the reader from one episode to the next, along the sequence of the narrative and along the string of words composing the text. Tradition equates the temporal stream, as well as the unfolding of a story, with a journey. It is therefore not arbitrary that the axis of combination be identified as a horizontal axis. By contrast, what Jakobson calls the *axis of selection*, or of equivalence, may be identified as a vertical axis. The disjunction makes a vertical crossing as well as a horizontal one.[23] A semantic crossing, a sort of metaphoric crossbreeding among themes, this "travessia" makes most of the major elements of the story at least partially equivalent, because of their common core—the disjunction itself.

The themes and motifs I am referring to are those that receive the most attention from the narrator: Diadorim, the devil, Hermógenes, the crossing, God, the *sertão*, and life. It is interesting that one of the means effectively used to suggest the equivalence of these elements is repeated patterns of sound, a factor we have already identified with the axis of selection or equivalence.[24] For example, Riobaldo says at one point, "eu ia denunciar nome, dar a cita: . . . *Satanão! Sujo!* . . . e dele disse somentes—*S* . . . —*Sertão* . . . *Sertão*" (p. 448). The equivalence of /s/, and particularly the sound similarity be-

tween "Satanão" and "sertão" suggests a parallel of two of the
work's main themes: the devil and the *sertão*. Riobaldo calls
Diadorim "Diá, Di" (p. 445), and refers to the devil by the
same apocopated form, "*diá*" (p. 33). Diadorim, "diabo,"
"diá"—common sounds promote the analysis of comparison
and contrast, which suggests a common semantic component.
These in turn tend to be identified with the theme of the
crossing or "travessia" by a sort of false etymology. The sequence "diá" as the common core of "Diadorim" and "diabo"
corresponds with the Greek root, "dia-," which means
"across." If the *sertão* and the devil are equal, then Diadorim,
the devil, the *sertão*, and the "travessia" are equal. Now,
through sound equality motifs so diametrically opposed as God
and the devil are semantically fused. The words "Deus" and
"demo" are placed in close proximity in various places: "Deus
ou o Demo" (p. 319); "De Deus? Do demo?" (p. 170); and "Ao
Demo ou a Deus" (p. 428). The repeated /de/ in itself highlights
equivalence; however, the fusion very subtly goes beyond that.
God and devil are in effect grafted into a common metaphorical
trunk, because of their common relationship of equality with a
single verb—"dar." Take the expression, "De déu em demos,
falseando" (p. 148). "Falseando" means "lying" and "going
amiss" or perhaps "taking a false step." "De déu em demos" is a
variation of the expression "de déu em déu," meaning also
"stumbling" or "reeling" ("déu" is a variant of "deu"). But sup-
pose we dislocate the *s* from one verb form to the other. Then
we get, "de deus em demo, falseando," which seems at least as
plausible, in a different sense, as what is written. The expression itself seems to "reel" between alternate meanings. In various passages we see this word play involving God or the devil
and some form of "dar": "Dou de. . . . De deus, do demo"
(p. 86); "o Arrenegado. . . Eu e ele—o Dê" (p. 372); "o Dado,
o Danado" (p. 318); and "Demos o Demo" (p. 394).

Besides this fusion of concepts created by sound play, there
is motivation for equating many of the important elements of

the work because of common features. Ambiguity itself is one of the features most responsible for this thematic crossing.

Diadorim is of course the incarnation of sexual ambiguity. It seems a bit unsatisfying in the context of the novel to say that Diadorim is a young woman disguised as a man. By realistic, worldly standards, it is extremely implausible that a beautiful woman could masquerade as a man among men and be un-detected. But plausibility by external standards is not the way of the novel. By definition in the work, Diadorim is a male on the outside and a female on the inside—a man with clothes on or a naked woman. She, when clothed, is he. The narrator's use of the pronouns "ele" and "ela" is consistent with this rule. In this manner, she is able to keep everyone including the first-time reader convinced of her manhood, on the basis of external evidence. He is able to convey to Riobaldo an extremely in-substantial impression of his womanhood, which is more ac-cessible to intuition than to empirical analysis.[25]

Hermógenes, another important character in the novel, is similarly cloaked in ambiguity. Did he or did he not make a pact with the devil? There is no question that he is an evil man. His treachery and violence bear that out well enough. But is the source of this evil from himself or from the evil one? An unsubstantiated rumor (how could it be otherwise?) that "O Hermógenes tem pauta. . . Ele se quis com o Capiroto" (p. 40) is all that suggests the pact. But much of his outward ap-pearance suggests he is just like any man:

> Estudei uma dúvida. Ao que será que seria o ser daquele homem tudo? Algum tinha referido que ele era casado, com mulher e filhos. Como podia? Ái-de vai, meu pensamento con-stante querendo entender a natureza dele, virada diferente de todas, a inocência daquela maldade. A qual me aluava. O Her-mógenes, numa casa, em certo lugar, com sua mulher, ele fazia festas em suas crianças pequenas, dava conselho, dava ensino. Daí saía. Feito lobisomem? (P. 179)

The ambiguity of Riobaldo's possible pact with the devil is
related to that of Hermógenes. By a bit of diabolic logic,
Riobaldo's agreement with the devil is necessary (and therefore
perhaps even justifiable) as a measure against Hermógenes'
pact. It is something like building an atom bomb to immobilize
the enemy's atom bomb. But if Hermógenes made no pact,
there is no justification for Riobaldo's. Besides the ambiguous
defensibility of Riobaldo's pact, there is ambiguity concerning
the accord itself. The actual moment of the possible pact involves the conflict between empirical evidence (or rather lack
thereof) and contradictory intuitive suggestion:

> —"Lúcifer! Lúcifer!..." — aí eu bramei, desengulindo.
> Não. Nada. . . .
> —"Lúcifer! Satanaz!..."
> Só outro silêncio. . . .
> —"Ei, Lúcifer! Satanaz, dos meus Infernos!"
> Voz minha se estragasse, em mim tudo era cordas e cobras. E
> foi aí. Foi. Ele não existe, e não apareceu nem respondeu—que
> é um falso imaginado. Mas eu supri que ele tinha me ouvido.
> Me ouviu, a conforme a ciência da noite e o envir de espaços,
> que medeia. (P. 319)

These particular cases of Diadorim, Riobaldo, and Hermógenes call universals into question. The existence or nonexistence of the devil is one of these universals, and a thematic
constant in the work. Riobaldo indicates his ambivalence in the
face of the matter by a cascade of contradictions: "O diabo
existe e não existe? Dou o dito" (p. 11); "o diabo não existe, não
há, e a ele eu vendi a alma" (p. 366); and "o Demônio mesmo
sabe que ele não há, só por só, que carece de existência"
(p. 354). The existence of the devil implies the existence of
God. Not only do both involve a spiritual existence, but in fact
one seems to exist in function of the other. In the Judeo-
Christian tradition, the concept of Satan is directly linked to

the word of God. So, although Riobaldo does not directly call
into question the existence of God, he does so by implication as
he questions the existence of God's counterpart. Riobaldo is in
an impossible position. Fearing the judgment of God, he questions the existence of Satan; this implies questioning the existence of God, but Riobaldo will *not* question that. Numerous
comments, such as "já perdi nele [no diabo] a crença, mercês a
Deus" (p. 10), reveal the position of reversible contradictions in
which he finds himself.

We encounter ambiguity as a common denominator of other
universals as well as God and the devil. The whole world fits the
pattern: "Ao que, este mundo é muito misturado" (p. 169).
Within the novel, the *sertão* equals the world: "O sertão é do
tamanho do mundo" (p. 59), and the *sertão* is also essentially
unsolvable: "Sertão é isto, o senhor sabe: tudo incerto, tudo
certo" (p. 121); and "O sertão é confusão em grande demasiado
sossego" (p. 343). We are continually told that living is "perigoso," for life has ambiguity at its core as well: "pois, no estado
do viver, as coisas vão enqueridas com muita astúcia: um dia é
todo para a esperança, o seguinte para a desconsolação"
(p. 310); and "a vida não é entendível" (p. 109).

The ambiguities within this novel are not as accessible to
analysis as many story-centered ambiguities, for intuition plays
a role in perceiving each of them. Ambiguity involves conflicting hypotheses that are equitenable. They may be so by the
same criteria, as when the text gives empirical clues supporting
each. Or, they may be equitenable by different criteria, for
example, one hypothesis may be supported by empirical evidence, and the other supported by intuitive evidence. Many of
Grande sertão: veredas' ambiguities are of this type. Concrete
evidence suggests that Diadorim is male, that Hermógenes
and Riobaldo have no agreement with the devil, and that spiritual beings like the devil and even God do not exist. But the
intangible yet undeniable voice of intuition suggests otherwise

to Riobaldo and to the reader. This intuitive hypothesis is more a given than the result of an accumulation of evidence.

The prominence of intuition as a substitute for concrete evidence brings the inquirer into the picture to a greater degree, because it is in terms of the subjective reactions of the inquirer that this intuitive evidence is established. In the novel, Riobaldo defines the ambiguity of the world by means of his more or less constant ambivalence vis-à-vis the world. "Eu nunca tinha certeza de coisa nenhuma" (p. 28), he admits. Faced with almost any circumstance, his response is about the same: "eu resguardava meu talvez" (p. 275). His actions reflect this ambivalence, and are almost predictable in their unpredictability. The *jagunços* in general define the unbiquitous ambiguity of the *sertão* by their constant ambivalent or contradictory behavior.[26] They hover between banditry and heroism, between honor and brutality. Their traitorous acts, their complicated, shifting alliances, and their zigzagging travels through the backlands are signals of uncertainty in an uncertain universe. One of the recurring songs in the novel seems to summarize the subject's response to the *sertão*'s ever-present enigma:

> Olererê, baiana. . .
> eu ia e não vou mais:—
> eu faço
> que vou
> lá dentro, o baiana,
> e volto do meio pra trás. . .
>
> (Pp. 54, 136, 341, 412)

Expressed in terms of a journey, the uncertainty of response takes the form of a change in directions: "eu ia e não vou mais;" and "volto do meio pra trás."

There is a specific dimension to this ambiguity that further serves to fuse motifs. The ambiguous elements often involve the idea of a reality *in layers*, with the outer layer obscuring what is underneath.

The notions of surface and depth, which have been so applicable to the other works studied, come into play again within the world of the backlands. According to Riobaldo's description, the hinterlands have their external dimension, which tends to hide something else underneath. He says that the *sertão* is apprehended superficially: "Porque o sertão se sabe só por alto" (p. 402), but that there is an occult dimension as well: "Só que o sertão é grande ocultado demais" (p. 382). He mentions various natural images from the backlands that reinforce the idea of a deceptive outward appearance, such as a manioc plant that looks like an edible variety, but is poisonous (p. 11), a beautiful flower with poisonous sap (p. 45), and an underground river (p. 222). People in the backlands have the same qualities. Sô Candelário is plagued with the idea of dormant, underlying leprosy, which "em qualquer hora . . . podia variar de aparecer" (p. 186). The starving *jagunços* unwittingly become cannibals, mistaking a boy for a monkey (p. 44). The placid, pious exterior of Maria Mutema hides the soul of a murderess (pp. 170–74).[27] And there is a bloodthirsty young boy with no apparent motive for his violent behavior. The spiritualist Quelemém suggests an underlying factor: that he is paying for atrocities committed in an earlier incarnation (pp. 13–14).

In the novel, life has its external reality, and an often contradictory reality below the surface: "Tem uma verdade que se carece de aprender, do encoberto, e que ninguém não ensina . . . a vida não é cousa terrível?" (p. 233). There is the evident life, but also the life "do que está reinando por debaixo" (p. 40).

The exterior component and its underlying counterpart are often opposites, often contradictory, but may nevertheless be inseparable. Riobaldo seems to define this inseparability of opposites, and the layered aspect they often assume, with his analogy of a waterfall:

> O diabo existe e não existe? . . . O senhor vê: existe cachoeira; e pois? Mas cachoeira é barranco de chão, e água se caindo por ele retombando; o senhor consome essa água, ou desfaz o barranco, sobra cachoeira alguma? Viver é negócio muito perigoso. . .
> (P. 11)

The waterfall is composed of superimposed opposites—rock and water. If one takes away either the water or the rock, the waterfall ceases to exist. It is the same with the major elements we have analyzed in the novel. With Riobaldo and Hermógenes there is a manifest dimension suggesting one thing, and something underneath suggesting the opposite. God and the devil, though opposites, seem to be layers of the same reality. Diadorim seems to be one thing on the inside and another on the outside. The garment hiding the other part of Diadorim is like the garment of language that tends to obscure part of the novel.[28] We should not forget that language, and in particular the language of this novel, has this stratified property and conforms to the analogy of the waterfall. Signifier and signified are the "água" and "barranco" of language. Take away one or the other, and there is no more language. And yet at times, although inseparable, the two do seem quite separate and even disparate.

This ambiguity of surface and depth is at the crux of the novel. It is essential to the more or less constant exclusive disjunction between the story's substance and the language's conspicuous style. This is a separating factor, dividing the reader's attention between form and content like so many bifurcations in a path, each requiring an unacceptable choice. Here we return to the idea of reading as a journey along a horizontal plane or axis. Riobaldo is at one point faced with the same sort of impossible bifurcation, and suggests a startling alternative:

"Qual é o caminho certo da gente? Nem para a frente nem para trás: só para cima" (p. 74). How is it that our hero on horseback can escape his horizontal ambiguities by going upwards? Other passages involving this verticality suggest there is some connection between going upwards and transcending the life of impossible choices. For example, the passage we saw earlier, "Porque o sertão se sabe só por alto," is equivocal. As we suggested before, it implies that the *sertão*, or life, is known only superficially by most people. However, it might signify as well that one gains knowledge of the *sertão*, from a high vantage point ("por alto" meaning literally "from above" instead of the more idiomatic "superficially"). Compadre Quelemém, who seems to have this privileged knowledge, takes this vertical approach. Riobaldo says, "Aprendi um pouco foi com o compadre meu Quelemém; . . . *quer não o caso inteirado em si, mas a sobre-coisa, a outra coisa*" (p. 152; my emphasis). Embodied in the idea of knowing something "por alto" is apprehending it without making many distinctions or divisions, with an orientation towards the general view instead of the details. It is a detached approach, more interested in the sameness existing between elements than in their differences. This ought to remind us of Jakobson's poetic function, where equivalence is projected into sequence. Appropriately, we have associated this metaphoric orientation with a vertical axis.

Ambiguity can highlight alternatives, and make us aware of differences. Or, it can itself be a structure that many different superstructures can have in common, and make us see sameness. In *Grande sertão: veredas*, we can perceive the disjunction of things as we follow the narrative from one enigma to the next, and deal with the narrative-bound distraction of conspicuous language. This is a "travessia" along a horizontal axis. But we can also see the *sameness* in so many of the novel's elements—*sertão*, life, devil, God, Diadorim, Hermógenes, etc. This approach in effect takes us above the sequential flow, and lets us see a pattern belonging simultaneously to most everything. That pattern, the unfolding of alternatives in itself, is the "matéria vertente" (p. 79) of the novel. The ambiguity that takes us along the horizontal line is also the form that permits, through metaphoric equivalence, the construction of the vertical line. The disjunction is the point of junction; the transversal moves towards the universal.

It should not be hard to see why a mystical character has been attributed to the book.[29] The novel's vision goes deep into the divisiveness of the universe, showing that "Regra do mundo é muito dividida" (p. 52), and reveals in this rule the overriding unity of the universe. When one reads the novel as a "travessia" through opposing directions, like a mystic, he gets the impression of a great union of opposites, of a "caosmos"[30] where things, because of their incompatibility, become ultimately compatible.

Epilogue

William Empson's *Seven Types of Ambiguity* (1930) made popular the idea that ambiguity may be a positive rather than negative factor in works of art. At the same time, it seems to have fostered the conception that there are several types of ambiguity, each somehow distinct from the others. If "ambiguity" is taken to mean "uncertainty" or "multiple meaning," then there are indeed several types of ambiguity; the taxonomy may in fact be infinite. Such a broadly defined concept, however, makes precise analysis difficult.

By the more narrow definition used in this study, there is only one fundamental type of ambiguity—what we have defined as the suggestion of two or more *mutually exclusive* propositions or meanings by means of a single expression. Using this definition, we find that a variety of ambiguous expressions may exist, with each case conforming to this single logical structure. Where classification might be appropriate is in an examination of the different types of *propositions* that may be involved in ambiguity. One relevant classification in the study of narrative is that of *representational* versus *nonrepresentational* propositions. The propositions in an ambiguous narrative may deal with what is represented, that is, some part of the story, or on the other hand the propositions may involve the perception of some conspicuous aspect in the presentation or expression itself.

On the basis of the four novels studied, we can conclude that ambiguity may exist entirely within the representational dimension of the narrative, as with *Dom Casmurro*; between what is represented and what represents, as with *Pedro Pá-*

151

ramo, Grande sertão: veredas, and *Cien años de soledad;* or
even within the nonrepresentational dimension, as with two of
the three reversible readings in *Pedro Páramo.*

I have not made extensive comparisons among the works,
and have especially avoided diachronic analysis aimed at suggesting influences or tracing development. One can hardly
provide a history of ambiguity on the basis of four novels. Nevertheless, a historical development is hinted at, which might
warrant further investigation. *Dom Casmurro* (1900), was published more than a half-century before any of the other works.
Its ambiguity is essentially representational, whereas the ambiguity in each of the other novels plays signified against signifier. In narrative, perhaps the latter tends to be more
characteristic of contemporary works.

Discussion of the novels has shown that ambiguity performs
several artistic functions. Its essential enigma often begs for a
solution, and thus draws the reader into intimate contact with
the message. The reader weighs alternatives, rereads certain
passages so as to justify them with seemingly conflicting evidence, and in general lingers over the text more than he might
were there no ambiguity.[1]

Ambiguity may be a means of making generalizations about
life. This function exists according to a mimetic tradition long
associated with narrative works. If books imitate life, then an
ambiguous book says something about the ambiguity of life.
One reads *Grande sertão: veredas* and gets the message that
living is dangerously ambiguous; he reads *Dom Casmurro,* and
gets a sense of an equivocal, mysterious, and perhaps treach-
erous world.

It may seem like a paradox in light of what I have just said,
but ambiguity is also a means of contrasting art and life. All the
novels analyzed involve an instability when we allow ourselves
to perceive a lifelike representation behind the medium of
expression. As long as we participate in the illusion that art is

life, we are torn between conflicting hypotheses. However, a stability may be reached if we acknowledge that art is a mechanism of illusion. For example, the impossible triangular drawing introduced at the beginning of the book is only impossible if we go along with the three-dimensional interpretation suggested. Seeing it instead as a series of lines in two dimensions (art, instead of life) allows for a completely stable perception.[2]

This is a radical change in attitudes, but one which art in general encourages.[3] Art calls attention to its artificiality. Because ambiguity suggests impossible situations, it seems especially able to foster this anti-illusionistic acknowledgment. Many of the claims for art's transcendental potential appear to be connected with this shift in perspective. Ambiguity functions effectively here as well. One takes the materials of the world, imitates them, and creates a situation that is in a worldly sense unstable and disturbing. But what is unstable in a real-life situation is stable if seen as an artifice. There is a disillusionment, both in the sense of frustration with the represented world, and in the sense of divesting oneself of illusion.

This plunge into the world in order to be transported out of the world has its similarities with mystical experience. Mystics often express themselves in logical contradictions. Their moment of transcendence involves rising above such intellectual categories and logical dichotomies, and perceiving the union of all things. As we saw in our study of *Cien años de soledad*, an affinity also exists between ambiguity and jokes. Jokes have a similar potential for transporting the mind, often abruptly, from one level of perception to another. The relationship between ambiguity, mysticism, and jokes in art might be profitably studied.

We can postulate all the functions attributed to ambiguity on the basis of our own reactions as we read the works, and on reasonable alternatives that any reader might choose in given textual circumstances. But the functions are also defined by the works themselves. Systems, it seems, tend to be recursive; that is, aspects of their substructures tend to mirror their superstructures, like Chinese boxes. I do not know how general a tendency this is, but it definitely applies to our four novels. The novels describe a fictional world. The fictional world in turn refers back to the narrative and describes the novels. For example, we have seen that the interplay between reader and text is metaphorically reproduced by the works. Bentinho, Juan Preciado, and Riobaldo all function like readers of an ambiguous text. The esthetic reactions of the reader are echoed in Bentinho's indecision and his being pulled into his love object's eyes. Juan Preciado's frustrated search for knowledge, and Riobaldo's constant hesitation and self-contradiction similarly suggest these reactions. Characters like Capitu, Susana San Juan, Diadorim, Remedios, la Bella, and Amaranta act like ambiguous texts. They are impenetrable, often in a sexual sense, but always in the sense of being mysterious. They convey contradictory messages, and alternately invite and repel those striving to commune with them.

Various natural images suggest the reader's vacillation between alternative hypotheses, such as the horse's midnight travels, back and forth, in Rulfo's novel, and the movement of the tide in Machado's. Others by portraying opposing currents or directions suggest ambiguity's crosscurrents of meaning. García Márquez' whirlwinds, Guimarães Rosa's bifurcating backlands, and Machado's undertow are examples.

Because of such multiple images of undecidability, ambiguity may have both a *disjunctive* and a *conjunctive* function.[4] On the one hand, ambiguity creates a counterpoint of opposing interpretations, a splitting of readings. On the other, the splitting itself can be a thematic unit and act as a common denominator for several aspects of a work, in effect tying disparate elements together. The analysis of *Grande sertão: veredas* suggests that the quality of undecidability, which creates an unstable impression as the reader progresses through the novel, ultimately creates a stable fictional universe because so many elements hold this quality in common and in effect become as one. Aspects of *Cien años de soledad*'s incomprehensible ending are mirrored in motifs throughout the work. Thus, the structure and function of incomprehensibility become, as it were, comprehensive. We have seen that a shift in perception allows us to stabilize representations that are ambiguous. The same kind of shift permits the stabilization of ambiguity's disjunction, so that it becomes a sign that may be employed like other signs to create greater meanings. While in one sense, ambiguity disturbs our sense of unity, in another, it may actually create that unified impression. It is a matter of levels. On a lower, more focused level, motifs are in disjunction, while on a higher level and from a more comprehensive perspective, the motif of undecidability consolidates disparate elements.

The fact that the novels are ambiguous, and self-consciously ambiguous as well, brings us back to one of those logical pitfalls described in the introductory chapter. We saw how certain self-referring paradoxes like the liar paradox ("I am lying") subject us to insoluble contradictions. We must assume the speaker is truthful to apprehend a lie, and assume he is lying to apprehend truth. Novels like the four studied here, which are ambiguous and by self-reference describe to us their ambiguity, seem to tell us something quite akin to the liar paradox. Each tells us, in effect, "I am indeterminate." When we try to document ambiguity and in the process discover how the works depict themselves as ambiguous works, we are forced into a reversibility of critical assumptions. The concept of a proposition or meaning underlying an expression presupposes determinacy. We proceed on this assumption, and find in the case of the novels not univocal propositions, but mutually exclusive ones, a discovery that causes us to favor the attitude of indeterminacy. Once we have posited this indeterminacy, however, motifs from the same novels come into view that seem to suggest to us in metaliterary language the very pattern of mutually exclusives. Again, this puts us in the mode favoring determinacy, until we realize that what is made explicit by the novel's self-reference is ambiguity itself. Given the paradoxical situation of works whose ambiguity is rather unambiguously described to us, our most appropriate reaction must be to waver endlessly between assumptions of determinacy and indeterminacy, between cognitive faith and skepticism.

Notes

Introduction

1. For example, see Edward W. Said, "Roads Taken and Not Taken in Contemporary Criticism," pp. 49–50.

2. An example of this position is Hazard Adams, "Contemporary Ideas of Literature: Terrible Beauty or Rough Beast?" pp. 58, 71–72.

3. Todorov defines the fantastic as a class of texts that prompt a hesitation between supernatural and natural interpretations. See Tzvetan Todorov, *Introduction à la littérature fantastique*, pp. 28–45.

4. See Thomas Colchie's amusing exploration of Jorge Luis Borges' influence upon Machado de Assis in "The Second-Best Horseman of the Apocalypse," pp. 63–68.

5. Jonathan Culler, "Issues in Contemporary American Critical Debate," pp. 1–18. All further references to this essay appear by parenthetical page numbers in the text.

6. This is implied in what he calls the "disappearance of the subject." See Culler, *Structuralist Poetics*, pp. 28–30, 118–19.

7. For a defense of literary propositions, see Gerald Graff, "Literature as Assertions," pp. 135–61.

8. An example in Hispanic criticism is David William Foster's *Studies in the Contemporary Spanish-American Short Story*. Foster, who clearly identifies his study with structuralism, stresses the inherent elusiveness and ambiguity of writing, and says his study "begins with the axiom that the impossibility of reductive meaning is an inherent feature of literary texts" (p. 5).

9. Carlos Fuentes, *La nueva novela hispanoamericana*, pp. 14–16.

10. See Gregory Rabassa, "Survival and Revival: The Baroque in Latin American Literature," pp. 59–65.

157

Chapter 1

1. L. S. Penrose and R. Penrose, "Impossible Objects: a Special Type of Visual Illusion," p. 31. M. C. Escher includes several variations of such impossible objects among his drawings. For example, see *The Graphic Work of M. C. Escher.*

2. Reproduced from E. H. Gombrich, "Illusion and Art," p. 239. The works of Salvador Dalí contain several more subtle examples of the same artifice. For instance, see "Slave Market with the Apparition of the Invisible Bust of Voltaire," in *Dalí.*

3. Shlomith Rimmon, *Concept of Ambiguity,* p. 3.

4. Ibid., p. 4.

5. Ibid., pp. 8–9.

6. Jorge Luis Borges, "El Sur," pp. 187–95.

7. Rimmon, *Concept of Ambiguity,* pp. 10–11.

8. Paul Valéry, *The Art of Poetry,* cited in Roman Jakobson, "Closing Statement: Linguistics and Poetics," p. 358.

9. Leonard Bernstein discusses this quality of language in *Unanswered Question,* pp. 211–14.

10. Ibid., pp. 39–41, 101–15, 186, 193–259.

11. Compare Max Black, *Critical Thinking,* p. 185; Irving M. Copi, *Introduction to Logic,* p. 92; and Philip Wheelwright, "On the Semantics of Poetry," in *Essays on the Language of Literature,* p. 252. Claude Gandelman, "The Metastability of Signs/Metastability as a Sign," pp. 83–105, discusses the same concept, where "two (or more) aspects . . . cannot be seen at one and the same time but only alternatively," and uses visual examples similar to those employed here. His name for the concept is "metastability" rather than "ambiguity." Tzvetan Todorov's definition of the fantastic in *Introduction à la littérature fantastique,* pp. 28–45, as hesitation between natural and supernatural explanations for events, is close to that used by Rimmon. By specifying particular qualities for mutually exclusive propositions, he makes the fantastic a kind of subset of ambiguous expressions in general. Several linguistic definitions of ambiguity agree with Rimmon's. For example, Noam Chomsky in *Language and Mind,* pp. 28–31, says ambiguous utterances are those that can have two or more nonequivalent underlying propositions. As chapter 2 explains, "nonequivalent" in the case of Chomsky's underlying struc-

NOTES TO CHAPTER 1

tures means practically the same thing as "mutually exclusive."

12. William Empson, *Seven Types of Ambiguity*, 2nd rev. ed. (New York: New Directions, 1947), p. 1.

13. Rimmon, *Concept of Ambiguity*, p. 17.

14. For further explanation of this transaction between perceiver and perceived, see Jules B. Davidoff, *Differences in Visual Perception*, pp. 131–66, and Douglas R. Hofstadter, *Gödel, Escher, Bach*, pp., 153–76.

15. Rimmon, *Concept of Ambiguity*, pp. 10–11.

16. The determinacy or nondeterminacy of textual meaning is of course the subject of considerable disagreement. See, for example, the individual discussions by Wayne Booth, M. H. Abrams, and J. Hillis Miller as listed in the Bibliography. There are profound philosophical questions involved in the polemic, with which I do not wish to become involved here. The disagreement probably attests to a dual nature of language, perhaps comparable to the corpuscular/wave duality perceived in the nature of light. Scientists have found it convenient to opt for one theory or the other, depending on the kind of analysis in which they are engaged. In the same way, regardless of philosophical questions, the choice of one theory of language or another may be made on the basis of which works better for a particular type of method. Admitting the possibility of determinate meaning is a practical necessity for this study's approach. We will see, however, that this exercise allows us glimpses of the other side of the nature of language. We will, in effect, treat conflicting readings as if each were univocal and supported by coherent evidence.

Logically, determinacy seems to be a sounder starting point than indeterminacy. As Rimmon-Kenan points out in "Deconstructive Reflections upon Deconstruction," pp. 185–88, even the insistence upon the universal indeterminacy of written texts crystallizes into a determinacy, and thus becomes subject to the oscillation of mutually exclusives. See also Hayden White's "The Absurdist Moment in Contemporary Literary Theory," p. 86, where he shows the "manifestly Absurd" position of writing interminably about the dissolution of writing.

17. Umberto Eco, "L'Oeuvre ouverte et la poétique de l'indétermination," p. 124.

18. This attitude, like so many of our ideas about art, is probably an

inheritance from Aristotle. See William Stanford, *Ambiguity in Greek Literature*, pp. 12–14.

19. Machado de Assis, *Memorial de Aires / O alienista*, p. 234.

20. Jacques Derrida, *La Dissémination*, p. 250.

21. Jan Mukařovsky, "Standard Language and Poetic Language," p. 19.

22. Rimmon, *Concept of Ambiguity*, pp. 234–35.

23. See, for example, Wilhelm Worringer's discussion of primitive man's attempt to transcend life's arbitrary reality by creating art based on geometric or stereometric forms uncommon in nature, in *Form in Gothic*, pp. 14–20.

Chapter 2

1. See, for example, Roland Barthes, "To Write: An Intransitive Verb?" p. 136; Foster, *Studies*, pp. 7–8; Culler, *Structuralist Poetics*, pp. 113–14, 205–24; Robert Scholes, *Structuralism in Literature*, pp. 17, 111–12.

2. Chomsky, *Language and Mind*, pp. 28–31.

3. For a review of the formalist and structuralist terms and their use by various theorists, see Rimmon, *Concept of Ambiguity*, pp. 28–34. The archetype/signature distinction is from Leslie Fiedler, "Archetype and Signature," pp. 40–47.

4. Rimmon, *Concept of Ambiguity*, pp. 32–34, distinguishes three degrees of depth in the structure of narrative: *fabula* (underlying story reduced to its essence), *sužet* (pre-medium artistic structure), and *discourse* (medium-bound artistic realization). In practice, it is normally not necessary to make a distinction between the latter two degrees. The deep/surface distinction is useful as a heuristic device but, like many attempts to systematize, has its limitations. See Barbara Herrnstein Smith, "Narrative Versions, Narrative Theories," pp. 313–36, for a critique of these theories.

5. See, for example, Eugênio Gomes, *O enigma de Capitu*, pp. 4–56. Gomes studies the following devices in *Dom Casmurro*: the narrator's exchanges with the reader, the narrator's references to his own writing process, hyperbole, ellipsis, colloquialisms, puns and other word plays, repetition, anecdotes, digressions, parody, aphorism,

21. Capitu's quite plausible explanation that D. Glória is either sick or jealous of Capitu for "taking Bentinho away from her" makes this clue ambiguous.

22. See Ana Lúcia Gazolla de Garcia, "Schopenhauer e Machado de Assis," pp. 327–34: "A visão apresentada é totalmente unilateral, e por conseguinte ambígua"; Coutinho, "Estudo introdutivo": "A conseqüência imediata dessa técnica [o uso do narrador-personagem] é a ambigüidade. . . . No caso de *Dom Casmurro* o leitor não vê nem acompanha os fatos. Simplesmente aceita o que Bentinho-Casmurro lhe conta, lhe consente ver"; and J. C. Kennear, "Machado de Assis: To Believe or Not to Believe," pp. 54–65: "*To believe or not to believe* . . . sums up one of the major differences between the novels of Machado's two periods: in the first, the narrator is to be believed, in the second [which includes *Dom Casmurro*] he is to be doubted at every turn."

23. Boris Tomashevsky, "Thematics," p. 68.

24. The idea of metaphor as a comparison between relationships, rather than simply a comparison between two elements, is from Chaim Perelman, *New Rhetoric and the Humanities*, pp. 91–93.

25. For a review of the most prominent critics' views, see Alberto I. Bagby, Jr., "Iaiá Garcia: More Optimism in Machado de Assis," *Inter-American Review of Bibliography*, 25 (1975), 271–84. Bagby takes exception to the thesis of pessimism; he states (p. 273): "Assis' world is not adverse, negative, unsympathetic or, as some have thought, even sadistic; it is merely neutral."

26. This is the case with Afrânio Coutinho in *A filosofia de Machado de Assis*, pp. 115–16, 197–98, and with Décio and Andreassi, "Retorno ao romance eterno," pp. 265–66.

27. For an overview of the traditional use of this sort of metaphor, see Ernst Robert Curtius, *European Literature and the Latin Middle Ages*, pp. 302–47.

28. Abraham Kaplan and Ernst Kris, "Esthetic Ambiguity," pp. 423–31.

29. Frank, "Introduction," pp. 10–11, calls attention to the "ressaca" as a metaphor for the novel.

30. Freud gives considerable attention to words and images or experiences that evoke contrary responses, in his lecture, "The 'Un-

canny,'" pp. 217–52. Capitu would certainly qualify as an "uncanny" woman in Freud's parlance. Freud connects uncanny phenomena with the castration complex; in a more general view, the uncanny might be tied to the fear of potency loss in other areas. The man's failure to fathom a woman's heart, or the reader's failure to detect meaning are areas that apply to *Dom Casmurro*.

Chapter 3

1. Gandelman, "The Metastability of Signs/Metastability as a Sign," p. 85.

2. Juan Rulfo, *Pedro Páramo*, p. 7. All further references to this work appear parenthetically within the text.

3. For a detailed discussion of Rulfo's ambiguous play with certain popular idioms, see María Luisa Bastos, "Clichés lingüísticos y ambigüedad en *Pedro Páramo*," pp. 31–44.

4. Todorov, *Introduction à la littérature fantastique*, pp. 35–36. Here I use the term "implied reader" differently from Wolfgang Iser in *The Implied Reader*. Iser defines the implied reader (p. xii) as the active participant who contributes to the composition of the work, after encountering the negation of certain social norms. In my usage the implied reader is more a definition of how to read than a challenge to create a new reading.

5. Luis Leal, "La estructura de *Pedro Páramo*," p. 287. See Leal's story review immediately following.

6. E. Kent Lioret, "A Matter of Life and Death in *Pedro Páramo*," pp. 99–102, provides not only an analysis of the life/death confusion, but also a review of diverging critical opinions.

7. For several other factors showing how Juan is uncertain about how and when he dies, see Lioret, "A Matter of Life and Death," pp. 101–2.

8. See John Brushwood, *Mexico in Its Novel*, p. 32.

9. Todorov, *Introduction à la littérature fantastique*, pp. 88–89.

10. See José de la Colina, "Susana San Juan (El mito femenino en *Pedro Páramo*)," pp. 20–21.

11. Hugo Rodríguez-Alcalá, *El arte de Juan Rulfo*, pp. 166–68.

12. See also Colina, "Susana San Juan (El mito femenino en *Pedro Páramo*)," p. 11.

13. See Ramón Díaz, "¿Dos Abundios en *Pedro Páramo?*" 6 Apr. 1969, p. 3; 13 Apr. 1969, p. 8.

14. For example, see Leal, "La estructura de *Pedro Páramo*," p. 287; Rodríguez-Alcalá, *El arte de Juan Rulfo*, p. 176; Manuel Ferrer Chivite, *El laberinto mexicano en/de Juan Rulfo*, pp. 35–36; and Mariana Frenk, "Pedro Páramo," p. 43.

15. Tomashevsky, "Thematics," p. 68.

16. Space dedicated to Juan Preciado in the novel is so disproportionate to his importance in the overall story that some have tended to separate the novel into two different stories—Juan Preciado's and Pedro Páramo's. See, for example, Violeta Peralta and Liliana Befumo Boschi, *Rulfo: la soledad creadora*, p. 100. Juan Preciado's account is so lacking in causality that it seems hardly to qualify as a story in the conventional sense.

17. Rodríguez-Alcalá, *El arte de Juan Rulfo*, p. 115.

18. Several writers have suggested that this sort of reading is appropriate. For example, Brushwood says that the reader "must unite with the novel, entering into the book and allowing the book to enter him. Once the subconscious is open, the reader's problem is solved" (*Mexico in Its Novel*, p. 32). Frenk says of the novel's language: "Es lacónica y expresiva. No describe, evoca. O, como Machado dice del verso: 'Presenta, no representa'" ("Pedro Páramo," p. 41). Rulfo himself has discouraged a representational reading, where individual characterization and clear logical distinctions are important, with statements such as "No hay límite entre el espacio y el tiempo," in Joseph Sommers, "Los muertos no tienen ni tiempo ni espacio: un dialogo de Juan Rulfo con Joseph Sommers," pp. 6–7; and "Es que Pedro Páramo no tiene rostro," in Roberto Vallarino, "'Pedro Páramo no tiene rostro': Rulfo," p. 16. The thesis of Didier T. Jaen's "La estructura lírica de 'Pedro Páramo'" is that "la estructura de *Pedro Páramo* obedece, más que a principios narrativos, a principios estructurales de la lírica" (p. 224).

19. Juan Rulfo, "Fragmento de la novela *Los murmullos*," pp. 6–7.

20. The idea for this analysis was suggested by Professor Merlin Compton of Brigham Young University, when he mentioned a term paper written on chiasmus in *Pedro Páramo* by Steven Nelson, a student. It was not possible to see the paper.

21. Bastos, "Clichés lingüísticos y ambigüedad en *Pedro Páramo*," pp. 32–33.

22. Gustavo Sainz discusses character-doubles in "¿Quién es Pedro Páramo?," p. 7. Sainz considers these character pairings to be consistent throughout the novel. In light of the comparisons established in the chiastic pattern, however, it seems possible that characters may have different doubles at different points in the novel.

Chapter 4

1. Smith, *Poetic Closure*, p. 152.

2. Ibid., pp. 158–95.

3. Gabriel García Márquez, *Cien años de soledad*, p. 347. All further page references to this work appear parenthetically within the text.

4. E. H. Gombrich uses Coleridge's term in his discussion of this reaction. See "Illusion and Art," pp. 193–217. See also Mary Louise Pratt's discussion of the "Cooperative Principle" in *Toward a Speech Act Theory of Literary Discourse*, especially pp. 152–58.

5. Rimmon, *Concept of Ambiguity*, pp. 5–8.

6. The impossible object shown here has actually been built with wood, and looks similar to the disconnected drawing here. Photographs with the proper perspective create the impression of an impossible connection. See J. O. Robinson, *The Psychology of Visual Illusion*, pp. 176, 181; and R. L. Gregory, "The Confounded Eye," pp. 87–88.

7. Mario Vargas Llosa's *García Márquez: historia de un deicidio* tends to fall into this category. The author assumes an equivalence between the manuscripts and the novel. The manuscripts, he says, "son la novela misma: Melquíades es el narrador de *Cien años de soledad*" (p. 541). However, he also talks about a change in the novel's point of view (exterior to interior), occurring when we find that Melquíades is author of the manuscripts. If the novel changes point of view, then according to his scheme by which the manuscripts "son la novela misma," the manuscripts must also have a change in point of view. Nevertheless, he quotes from the novel itself to show that the manuscript is "la historia de Macondo y de la familia '*escrito por*

*Melquíades hasta en sus detalles más triviales con cien años de antici-
pación'"* (p. 540, *Cien años de soledad,* p. 349).

Commenting on the self-extinguishing ending, Vargas Llosa says,
"La estructura refleja la gran ambición de la materia: describir una
realidad hasta agotarla, ser su propio principio y fin" (p. 543). Apparently not satisfied with the idea of a novel that writes itself out of
existence, he offers the disclaimer, "Esta novela que se agota en sí
misma es, al mismo tiempo, como toda gran creación, un objeto
'inagotable,' dotado de una vida propia, siempre en proceso de trans-
formación, de reflejo y negación de esa realidad real también en
perpetua mudanza" (p. 615).
8. Emir Rodríguez Monegal, "Novedad y anacronismo en 'Cien
años de soledad,'" acknowledges that Melquíades' manuscript "es, de
alguna manera, la misma novela que hemos leído y recorrido de la
mano de García Márquez" (p. 18). He senses the impossible situation
this equivalence creates in conjunction with the storm. Although he
does not express the thought directly, he appears at least to feel that
the novel's existence is the ultimate "anacronismo" of its contents,
and deals with it thusly:

> Cuando Aureliano el bastardo recorre a saltos el libro de Mel-
> quíades para buscar la fecha exacta y las circunstancias de su
> muerte, mientras afuera de ese cuarto mágico, ese recinto in-
> tocable, esa zona sagrada, el viento arrasa para siempre con
> Macondo, Aureliano ha descubierto (tal vez sin entenderlo del
> todo) que está a salvo de las destrucciones del tiempo, porque él
> no vive ya en el tiempo, porque en realidad no ha vivido nunca
> en el tiempo, porque de hecho siempre ha vivido en otra di-
> mensión: la del espejismo de Macondo. Espejismo hecho de
> soledad y muerte, pero hecho sobre todo de la inmortalidad que
> confiere la palabra. (P. 19)

Rodríguez Monegal's resolution of *Cien años de soledad* requires a
shift to another dimension. This having been effected, Aureliano (and
by extension the other characters) belong within the "cuarto mág-
ico, . . . recinto intocable" of a book. He expresses the same idea in
"*One Hundred Years of Solitude:* The Last Three Pages," pp. 484–89.
Doris Rolfe, another critic who senses the ambiguous structure

involved, calls the work's ending "el énfasis final y definitivo para expresar que la novela es ficción." See "Tono y estructura en *Cien años de soledad*," p. 261. See also Susana Cordero de Espinosa, "*Cien años de soledad*: un asesinato del olvido," pp. 201–27, and Vargas Llosa, *García Márquez*, pp. 544–45.

9. Gombrich, "Illusion and Art," pp. 193–94.

10. Aleyda Roldán de Micolta, "*Cien años de soledad*: una novela construida sobre espejos," p. 239. See also Rodríguez Monegal, "*One Hundred Years of Solitude*," pp. 486, 489.

11. William L. Siemens, "Tiempo, entropía y la estructura de *Cien años de soledad*," p. 360.

12. Gombrich, "Illusion and Art," p. 208.

13. In particular, a work may accomplish this by implicitly defining the function of its reader. See Todorov, *Introduction à la littérature fantastique*, p. 35–36.

14. M. H. Abrams, *El espejo y la lámpara: teoría romántica y tradición crítica*, pp. 59–86.

15. Roldán de Micolta, "*Cien años de soledad*," pp. 239–57; Suzanne Jill Levine, *El espejo hablado: un estudio de "Cien años de soledad*," pp. 127–49.

16. See Hofstadter's discussion of "strange loops" in *Gödel, Escher, Bach*, pp. 10–22.

17. Levine, *El espejo hablado*, pp. 107–25; Rolfe, "Tono y estructura en *Cien años de soledad*," p. 276.

18. Vargas Llosa, *García Márquez*, p. 550.

19. Ibid., p. 551.

20. See J. Hillis Miller, "Ariadne's Thread: Repetition and the Narrative Line," pp. 55–77; Rimmon-Kenan, "The Paradoxical Status of Repetition," pp. 151–59; and Octavio Paz, *Corriente alterna*, pp. 69–75. For specific mention of ambiguous linearity in the novel, see Edelweis Serra, "Narrema e isotopía en *Cien años de soledad*," p. 332; and Juan Antonio Castro, "La línea recta y el laberinto de García Márquez," p. 24. Castro simply equates linearity with traditional, easy-to-follow narrative and the labyrinth with its opposite, calling the author's narrative style "difícilmente fácil," and "al mismo tiempo lineal y laberíntico."

21. Rodríguez Monegal, "Novedad," pp. 16–17.

22. María A. Salgado, "¿'Civilización y barbarie' o 'Imaginación y

barbarie'?" p. 304; Rolfe, "Tono y estructura en *Cien años de soledad*," pp. 265–69, 275; Roldán de Micolta, *"Cien años de soledad*," p. 247; Serra, "Narrema e isotopía en *Cien años de soledad*," pp. 336–39; Vargas Llosa, *García Márquez*, pp. 585–607.

23. Mircea Eliade, *The Myth of the Eternal Return, or, Cosmos and History*, pp. 3–48. See also Luce López-Baralt's discussion of the novel's characters' return to infancy, "Algunas observaciones sobre el rescate artístico de la niñez en 'Cien años de soledad' y 'El tambor de hojalata,'" pp. 55–67.

24. Siemens, "Tiempo, entropía y la estructura de *Cien años de soledad*," pp. 362–65.

25. Sigmund Freud, *Jokes and Their Relation to the Unconscious*, pp. 197–98. See also John Allen Paulos' discussion of abrupt reversals in *Mathematics and Humor*, pp. 75–101.

26. According to this partial reading, the novel's title is ironic, because solitude along with everything else in a similar vein is invalidated. Only a few critics have seen something besides unequivocal solitude in the novel. See Cordero de Espinosa, *"Cien años de soledad*," p. 227, and María Luisa Mendoza, "100 años de compañia." Even the notion of one hundred years, supposedly delimiting the temporal existence of Macondo, is equivocal. See pages 69, 138, and 165 for references suggesting that more than one hundred years are involved.

27. See, for example, Vargas Llosa, *García Márquez*, pp. 498–528.

28. In interviews, García Márquez seems to have encouraged the reading of *Cien años de soledad* as a sort of joke. For example, in Miguel Fernández-Braso, *Gabriel García Márquez: una conversación infinita*, pp. 74, 82, he insists that writing the novel was a continually laughable experience and that the work is totally lacking in seriousness. Such statements are of course hopelessly ambiguous. Should we take someone seriously who insists his work is not to be taken seriously?

Chapter 5

1. João Guimarães Rosa, *Grande sertão: veredas*. All further references to this novel will be by parenthetical page numbers in the text.

2. It might seem like forcing things to call attention to configurations of letters, if the author did not do the same within the novel. At one point, Riobaldo refers to himself as "o ypsilone dum jegue . . . cabeça orelhamente" (p. 432). He describes the head of an ass in terms of a Y, but the context shows that he also seems to be using the image, similar to the V in its disjunction, to suggest his indecision.

3. For example, see Mary L. Daniel, "Word Formation and Deformation in *Grande sertão: veredas*," pp. 81–97; Mary L. Daniel, *João Guimarães Rosa: travessia literária*; Nei Leandro de Castro, *Universo e vocabulário do grande sertão*; M. Cavalcanti Proença, "Alguns aspectos formais de *Grande sertão: veredas*," pp. 8–12; and Ivana Versiani's study of the subjective in the novel, in Nelly Novaes Coelho and Ivana Versiani, *Guimarães Rosa: dois estudos*, pp. 79–140.

4. Jon S. Vincent, *João Guimarães Rosa*, p. 65. Vincent supports his claim that the novel is not plotless by providing, immediately following this citation, a summary of the novel's action.

5. Ralph Freedman, *The Lyrical Novel*, p. 1.

6. Among these are Adolfo Casais Monteiro, Henriqueta Lisboa, Autran Dourado, Ivana Versiani, and Euryalo Cannabrava. See Vincent, *João Guimarães Rosa*, pp. 64, 70, 165–66; and Castro, *Universo e vocabulário do grande sertão*, p. 5.

7. João Guimarães Rosa, *Seleta de João Guimarães Rosa*, pp. 58–64.

8. See Henriqueta Lisboa, "A poesia de *Grande sertão: veredas*," pp. 141–46; Maria Luísa Ramos, "O elemento poético em *Grande sertão: veredas*," pp. 53–75; Mary L. Daniel's chapter on poetics and rhetoric, *João Guimarães Rosa*, pp. 137–67; and Pedro Xisto, "À busca da poesia," pp. 7–39.

9. Proença's study, one of the most extensive ones exclusively on *Grande sertão: veredas*, gives copious examples of most of these devices. In the numbered paragraphs, all underlines are added.

10. In a letter to Harriet de Onis, who translated the novel into English, Guimarães Rosa wrote, "Nos meus livros . . . tem importância, pelo menos igual ao do sentido da estória, se é que não muito mais: a poética ou poeticidade da forma, tanto a 'sensação' mágica, visual, das palavras, quanto a 'eficácia sonora' delas; e mais as al-

terações viventes do ritmo, a música subjacente, as fórmulas esqueletos das frases—transmitindo ao subconsciente vibrações emotivas subtis." See Daniel, *João Guimarães Rosa*, p. 172.

11. See Hofstadter's discussion of holism vs. reductionism in *Gödel, Escher, Bach*, pp. 310–36.

12. Daniel, *João Guimaraes Rosa*, pp. 175–76, writes: "Na sua preocupação com o conteúdo e com a forma das suas obras, Guimarães Rosa faz esta colega e não escrava daquele; ou, melhor dito, na obra rosiana não se separam os dois elementos mas se efetua uma confluência deles." Augusto de Campos says in "Um lance de 'dês' do grande sertão," p. 5, "em Guimarães Rosa nada ou quase nada parece haver de gratuito. As mais ousadas invenções lingüísticas estão sempre em relação com o conteúdo."

13. Jean Cohen, *Estructura del lenguaje poético*, p. 74.

14. Ibid., p. 96.

15. Ibid., pp. 96–97.

16. Ibid., p. 97.

17. Jakobson, "Closing Statement," p. 353.

18. Ibid., p. 356.

19. Ibid. p. 367. Here the author borrows the term "figure of sound" from Gerard Manley Hopkins.

20. Jakobson, "Closing Statement," p. 358.

21. Ibid., p. 357; Cohen, *Estructura del lenguaje poético*, pp. 9–14. For a critique of the idea of a dichotomy between "poetic" and "ordinary" language, see Mary Louise Pratt, *Toward a Speech Act Theory*, pp. 3–37.

22. Claude Gandelman concurs with this opinion in "Metastability of Signs," pp. 94–96. According to him, signifier and signified are reversible in the way in which ambiguous figure-ground drawings are reversible. That is, when we perceive one, the other in effect dissolves.

23. José Carlos Garbuglio, *O mundo movente de Guimarães Rosa*, pp. 21–49, sees a similar pattern, what he calls "a estrutura bipolar da narrativa." Rather than placing the metaphoric process along the vertical axis, however, he places on it a metalinguistic process, identified as Riobaldo's constant reflections as narrator upon the act of narrating.

24. Many of the following examples showing how sound equivalence promotes semantic fusion are to be found in Augusto de Campos, "Um lance de 'dês' do grande sertão," pp. 5–7.

25. The ending "-im" in "Diadorim" is a truncated form of either "-inho," "-ino," "-inha," or "-ina," making the character's name well suited for this sexual ambiguity. See Daniel, *João Guimarães Rosa*, pp. 49–50.

26. This is perhaps the main point of Walnice Nogueira Galvão's *As formas do falso: um estudo sobre a ambigüidade no* Grande sertão: veredas. Galvão's study stresses the ambiguity of the *jagunço* as a reflection of social conditions. See also Antônio Cândido, "O sertão e o mundo," p. 5; and Vera Lúcia Andrade, "Conceituação de jagunço e jagunçagem em *Grande sertão: veredas*," pp. 6–7.

27. Galvão, in *As formas do falso*, points out the importance of layers, calling the concept "a coisa dentro da outra." She sees the tale of Maria Mutema as a central anecdote "dentro de outra," which in itself defines the theme of ambiguity in layers. See pp. 117–32.

28. Jakobson, in "Closing Statement," uses this same type of analogy. On page 374, he says that in some literary forms, "verbal devices are unostentatious and language seems a nearly transparent garment. But one must say with Charles Sanders Peirce: 'This clothing can never be completely stripped off, it is only changed for something more diaphanous.'" Of course both this analogy and the veil analogy mentioned earlier have a layered dimension. The only difference is that in one the object *wears* the veil. Diadorim's clothing is surely thicker than a veil, and the novel's language is correspondingly conspicuous and opaque. Incidentally, the *Oxford English Dictionary* shows one name for a veil-like curtain, such as that in our analogy, to be "traverse," the etymologic brother of "travessia." Compare also the similarity of "travesti" as it refers to Diadorim's disguise, and "travessia."

29. See Francisco Faus, "João Guimarães Rosa, le 'contemplatif transparent,'" pp. 61–70.

30. A. Sérgio Bueno uses this word to describe the coexistence of chaos and harmony in the novel: "A narrativa cristaliza um estado de transitoriedade." See "A narrativa como caosmos: o medo e o amor em 'Grande sertão: veredas,'" pp. 6–7.

Epilogue

1. Rimmon discusses effects of ambiguity on the reader, especially in light of formalist and structuralist theories, in *Concept of Ambiguity*, pp. 228–31.

2. For further discussion of this reaction, see Gandelman, "Metastability of Signs," pp. 89–91, and Hofstadter, *Gödel, Escher, Bach*, pp. 461–79.

3. See Rimmon, *Concept of Ambiguity*, p. 231.

4. "Conjunctive function" here should not be confused with what Kaplan and Kris call "conjunctive ambiguity" in "Esthetic Ambiguity," p. 419. Their term refers to multiple meanings that are effective simultaneously and require no choice among them. Their "conjunctive ambiguity" does not qualify as ambiguity by our definition.

Bibliography

Primary Sources

Assis, Machado de. *Dom Casmurro*. In *Obra completa*. Vol. 1. Ed. Afrânio Coutinho. Rio de Janeiro: Editora José Aguilar, 1959.

———. "Eça de Queirós: *O primo Basílio*." In *Obra completa*. Vol. 3. Ed. Afrânio Coutinho, pp. 903–13. Rio de Janeiro: Editora José Aguilar, 1962.

———. *Memorial de Aires / O alienista*. 2d ed. Ed. Massaud Moisés. São Paulo: Editora Cultrix, 1963.

Borges, Jorge Luis. "El Sur." In *Obras completas*. Vol. 5, pp. 187–95. Buenos Aires: Emecé Editores, 1954.

García Márquez, Gabriel. *Cien años de soledad*. Buenos Aires: Editorial Sudamericana, 1971.

Rosa, João Guimarães. *Grande sertão: veredas*. Rio de Janeiro: José Olympio, 1976.

———. *Seleta de João Guimarães Rosa*. Ed. Paulo Rónai. Rio de Janeiro: José Olympio, 1973.

Rulfo, Juan. "Fragmento de la novela *Los murmullos*." *Universidad de México* 8, no. 10 (1954): 6–7.

———. *Pedro Páramo*. Mexico City: Fondo de Cultura Económico, 1964.

General and Theoretical Sources

Abrams, M. H. "The Deconstructive Angel." *Critical Inquiry* 3 (1977): 425–38.

———. *El espejo y la lámpara: teoría romántica y tradición crítica*. Trans. Meliton Bustamante. Barcelona: Barral Editores, 1974.

Adams, Hazard. "Contemporary Ideas of Literature: Terrible Beauty or Rough Beast?" In *Directions for Criticism: Structuralism and its Alternatives*, ed. Murray Krieger and L. S. Dembo, pp. 55–83. Madison: Univ. of Wisconsin Press, 1977.

Barthes, Roland. "To Write: An Intransitive Verb?" In *The Struc-turalist Controversy: The Languages of Criticism and the Sciences of Man*, ed. Richard Macksey and Eugenio Donato, pp. 155–67. Baltimore: Johns Hopkins University Press, 1972.

Beardsley, Monroe. *Aesthetics: Problems in the Philosophy of Crit-icism*. New York: Harcourt, Brace & World, 1958.

Bernstein, Leonard. *The Unanswered Question: Six Talks at Har-vard*. Cambridge: Harvard University Press, 1976.

Black, Max. *Critical Thinking: An Introduction to Logic and Scien-tific Method*. 2d ed. New York: Prentice Hall, 1952.

Booth, Wayne C. "'Preserving the Exemplar': or, How Not to Dig Our Own Graves." *Critical Inquiry* 3 (1977): 407–23.

Chomsky, Noam. *Language and Mind*. Enl. ed. New York: Harcourt, Brace & Jovanovich, 1972.

Cohen, Jean. *Estructura del lenguaje poético*. Trans. Martín Blanco Álvarez. Madrid: Editorial Gredos, 1974.

Copi, Irving M. *Introduction to Logic*. 2d ed. New York: Macmillan, 1961.

Culler, Jonathan. "Issues in Contemporary American Critical De-bate." In *American Criticism in the Poststructuralist Age*, ed. Ira Konigsberg, pp. 1–18. Ann Arbor: Michigan Studies in the Hu-manities, 1981.

———. *Structuralist Poetics: Structuralism, Linguistics and the Study of Literature*. Ithaca, N.Y.: Cornell University Press, 1975.

Curtius, Ernst Robert. *European Literature and the Latin Middle Ages*. Trans. Willard R. Trask. New York: Harper & Row, 1953.

Dalí, Salvador. *Dalí*. Ed. David Larkin. New York: Ballantine, 1974.

Davidoff, Jules B. *Differences in Visual Perception: The Individual Eye*. New York: Academic Press, 1975.

Derrida, Jacques. *La Dissémination*. Paris: Éditions du Seuil, 1972.

Eco, Umberto. "L'Oeuvre ouverte et la poétique de l'indétermina-tion." Trans. André Boucourechliev. *La Nouvelle Revue Française* 8 (1960): 117–24, 313–20.

Eliade, Mircea. *The Myth of the Eternal Return, or, Cosmos and History*. Trans. Willard R. Trask. Princeton: Princeton University Press, 1954.

Empson, William. *Seven Types of Ambiguity*. 2d rev. ed. New York: New Directions, 1947.

Escher, M. C. *The Graphic Works of M. C. Escher.* New York: Ballantine, 1971.

Fiedler, Leslie. "Archetype and Signature." In *Symbol and Myth in Modern Literature*, ed. F. Parvin Sharpless, pp. 40–47. Rochelle Park, N.J.: Hayden, 1976.

Foster, David William. *Studies in the Contemporary Spanish-American Short Story.* Columbia: University of Missouri Press, 1979.

Freedman, Ralph. *The Lyrical Novel: Studies in Herman Hesse, André Gide, and Virginia Wolf.* Princeton: Princeton University Press, 1963.

Freud, Sigmund. *Jokes and Their Relation to the Unconscious.* Trans. and ed. James Strachey. New York: W. W. Norton, 1960.

———. "The 'Uncanny.'" In *Complete Psychological Works of Sigmund Freud.* Vol. 17. Trans. James Strachey, pp. 217–52. London: Hogarth Press, 1962.

Fuentes, Carlos. *La nueva novela hispanoamericana.* Mexico City: Joaquín Moritz, 1969.

Gandelman, Claude. "The Metastability of Signs/Metastability as a Sign." *Semiotica* 28 (1979): 83–105.

Gombrich, E. H. "Illusion and Art." In *Illusion in Nature and Art*, ed. R. L. Gregory and E. H. Gombrich, pp. 193–243. New York: Charles Scribner's Sons, 1973.

Graff, Gerald. "Literature as Assertions." In *American Criticism in the Poststructuralist Age*, ed. Ira Konigsberg, pp. 135–61. Ann Arbor: Michigan Studies in the Humanities, 1981.

Gregory, R. L. "The Confounded Eye." In *Illusion in Nature and Art*, ed. R. L. Gregory and E. H. Gombrich, pp. 48–95. New York: Charles Scribner's Sons, 1973.

Hofstadter, Douglas R. *Gödel, Escher, Bach: An Eternal Golden Braid.* New York: Basic Books, 1979.

Iser, Wolfgang. *The Implied Reader: Patterns of Communication in Prose Fiction from Bunyan to Beckett.* Baltimore: Johns Hopkins University Press, 1974.

Jakobson, Roman. "Closing Statement: Linguistics and Poetics." In *Style in Language*, ed. Thomas A. Sebeok, pp. 350–77. N.p.: Technology Press of Massachusetts Institute of Technology and John Wiley and Sons, 1960.

Kaplan, Abraham, and Ernst Kris. "Esthetic Ambiguity." *Philosophy and Phenomenological Research* 8 (1948): 415–35.

Miller, J. Hillis. "Ariadne's Thread: Repetition and the Narrative Line." *Critical Inquiry* 3 (1976): 57–77.

———. "The Critic as Host." *Critical Inquiry* 3 (1977): 439–47.

Mukařovsky, Jan. "Standard Language and Poetic Language." In *A Prague School Reader on Esthetics, Literary Structure, and Style*, ed. and trans. Paul L. Garvin, p. 17–30. Washington, D.C.: Georgetown University Press, 1964.

Paulos, John Allen. *Mathematics and Humor*. Chicago: University of Chicago Press, 1980.

Paz, Octavio. *Corriente alterna*. Mexico City: Siglo Veintiuno Editores, 1967.

Penrose, L. S., and R. Penrose. "Impossible Objects: A Special Type of Visual Illusion." *The British Journal of Psychology* 49 (1958): 31–33.

Perelman, Chaim. *The New Rhetoric and the Humanities: Essays on Rhetoric and its Applications*. Dordrecht, Holland: D. Riedel, 1979.

Pratt, Mary Louise. *Toward a Speech Act Theory of Literary Discourse*. Bloomington: Indiana University Press, 1977.

Rabassa, Gregory. "Survival and Revival: The Baroque in Latin American Literature." *Luso-Brazilian Review* 15 (1978 suppl.): 59–65.

Rimmon, Shlomith. *The Concept of Ambiguity—the Example of James*. Chicago: University of Chicago Press, 1977.

Rimmon-Kenan, Shlomith. "Deconstructive Reflections on Deconstruction: In Reply to Hillis Miller." *Poetics Today* 2, no. 1b (1980–81): 185–88.

———. "The Paradoxical Status of Repetition." *Poetics Today* 1, no. 4 (1980): 151–59.

Robinson, J. O. *The Psychology of Visual Illusion*. London: Hutchinson University Library, 1972.

Said, Edward W. "Roads Taken and Not Taken in Contemporary Criticism." In *Directions for Criticism: Structuralism and its Alternatives*, ed. Murray Krieger and L. S. Dembo, pp. 33–54. Madison: University of Wisconsin Press, 1977.

Scholes, Robert. *Structuralism in Literature: An Introduction*. New Haven, Conn.: Yale University Press, 1974.

Smith, Barbara Herrnstein. "Narrative Versions, Narrative Theories." *Critical Inquiry* 7 (1980): 313–36.

————. *Poetic Closure: A Study of How Poems End*. Chicago: University of Chicago Press, 1968.

Stanford, William Bedel. *Ambiguity in Greek Literature: Studies in Theory and Practice*. 1939. Reprint. New York: Johnson Reprint, 1972.

Todorov, Tzvetan. *Introduction à la littérature fantastique*. Paris: Éditions du Seuil, 1970.

Tomashevsky, Boris. "Thematics." In *Russian Formalist Criticism: Four Essays*, trans. and ed. Lee T. Lemon and Marion D. Reis, pp. 61–95. Lincoln: University of Nebraska Press, 1965.

Wheelwright, Philip. "On the Semantics of Poetry." In *Essays on the Language of Literature*, ed. Seymour Chatman and Samuel R. Levin, pp. 250–63. New York: Houghton Mifflin, 1967.

White, Hayden. "The Absurdist Moment in Contemporary Literary Theory." In *Directions for Criticism: Structuralism and its Alternatives*, ed. Murray Krieger and L. S. Dembo, pp. 85–110. Madison: University of Wisconsin Press.

Worringer, Wilhelm. *Form in Gothic*. Trans. Herbert Read. New York: Schocken, 1957.

Sources on Machado's Work

Bagby, Alberto I., Jr. "Iaiá Garcia: More Optimism in Machado de Assis." *Inter-American Review of Bibliography* 25 (1975): 271–84.

Brayner, Sônia. "O texto e o jogo das máscaras." *Minas Gerais* (Lit. Suppl.) 17 Jan. 1976, pp. 1–2.

Carvalho Filho, Aloysio de. *O processo penal de Capitu*. Salvador: Imprensa Regina, n.d.

Colchie, Thomas. "The Second-Best Horseman of the Apocalypse." *Review* 75 16 (1975): 63–68.

Coutinho, Afrânio. "Estudo introdutivo." In Machado de Assis, *Dom Casmurro*. N.p.: Edições de Ouro, n.d.

————. *A filosofia de Machado de Assis e outros ensaios*. Rio de Janeiro: Livraria São José, 1959.

Décio, João, and Lurdes Andreassi. "Retorno ao romance eterno: *D. Casmurro* de Machado de Assis." *Ocidente* no. 410 (1972): 257–69.

Ellis, Keith. "Technique and Ambiguity in 'Dom Casmurro.'" *Hispania* 45 (1965): 76–81.

Frank, Waldo. "Introduction." In Machado de Assis, *Dom Casmurro*. Trans. Helen Caldwell. New York: Noonday Press, 1953, pp. 5–13.

García, Ana Lúcia Gazolla de. "Schopenhauer e Machado de Assis." *Romance Notes* 19, no. 3 (1979): 327–34.

Gomes, Eugênio. *O enigma de Capitu: ensaio de interpretação*. Rio de Janeiro: José Olympio, 1967.

Jacques, Alfredo. *Machado de Assis: equívocos da crítica*. Porto Alegre: Editora Movimento, 1974.

Kennear, J. C. "Machado de Assis: To Believe or Not to Believe." *Modern Language Review* 71 (1976): 54–65.

MacAdam, Alfred J. *Modern Latin American Narratives: The Dreams of Reason*. Chicago: University of Chicago Press, 1977.

Martins, Wilson. "Pro or Contra in Casmurro." Trans. Peter Lownds. *Review 75* 16 (1975): 60–63.

Sources on Rulfo's Work

Bastos, María Luisa. "Clichés lingüísticos y ambigüedad en *Pedro Páramo*." *Revista Iberoamericana* 102–03 (1978): 31–44.

Befumo Boschi, Liliana. "*Pedro Páramo*: la búsqueda del espacio y de la palabra." *Atenea* no. 432 (1975): 213–30.

Brushwood, John. *Mexico in Its Novel: A Nation's Search for Identity*. Austin: University of Texas Press, 1966.

Colina, José de la. "Susana San Juan (El mito femenino en *Pedro Páramo*)." *Universidad de México* 29, no. 8 (1965): 19–21.

Díaz, Ramón. "¿Dos Abundios en *Pedro Páramo*?" *Diario de la Cultura* 6 Apr. 1969, p. 3; 13 Apr. 1969, p. 8.

Ferrer Chivite, Manuel. *El laberinto mexicano en/de Juan Rulfo*. Mexico City: Editorial Novaro, 1972.

Frenk, Mariana. "Pedro Páramo." In *La narrativa de Juan Rulfo: interpretaciones críticas*. Ed. Joseph Sommers, pp. 31–43. Mexico City: Sep/Setentas, 1974.

Jaén, Didier T. "La estructura lírica de 'Pedro Páramo.'" *Revista Hispánica Moderna* 33 (1967): 224–31.

Leal, Luis. "La estructura de *Pedro Páramo*." *Anuario de Letras* 4 (1964): 287–94.

Lioret, E. Kent. "A Matter of Life and Death in *Pedro Páramo*." *Romance Notes* 17 (1976): 99–102.

Peralta, Violeta, and Liliana Befumo Boschi. *Rulfo: la soledad creadora*. Buenos Aires: Fernando García Cambeiro, 1975.

Rodríguez-Alcalá, Hugo. *El arte de Juan Rulfo*. Mexico City: Instituto Nacional de Bellas Artes, 1965.

Sainz, Gustavo. "¿Quién es Pedro Páramo?" *La Onda* (Lit. Suppl. to *Novedades*) 27 Apr.–3 May 1975, p. 7.

Sommers, Joseph. "Los muertos no tienen ni tiempo ni espacio: un diálogo de Juan Rulfo con Joseph Sommers." *La Cultura en Mexico* (Lit. Suppl. to ¡*Siempre!*) 16 Aug. 1973, pp. 5–7.

Vallarino, Roberto. "'Pedro Páramo no tiene rostro': Rulfo." *Uno Más Uno* 20 Sept. 1978, p. 16.

Sources on García Márquez' Work

Castro, Juan Antonio. "La línea recta y el laberinto de García Márquez." *Ya* (Madrid) 21 May 1969, p. 24.

Espinosa, Susana Cordero de. "*Cien años de soledad:* un asesinato del olvido." In *Lectura de García Márquez: doce estudios*. Ed. Manuel Corrales Pascual, pp. 201–27. Quito: Centro de Publicaciones de la Pontificia Universidad Católica del Ecuador, 1975.

Fernández Braso, Miguel. *Gabriel García Márquez, una conversación infinita*. Madrid: Editorial Azur, 1969.

Levine, Suzanne Jill. *El espejo hablado: un estudio de "Cien años de soledad."* Caracas: Monte Ávila Editores, n.d.

López-Baralt, Luce. "Algunas observaciones sobre el rescate artístico de la niñez en 'Cien años de soledad' y 'El tambor de hojalata.'" *Sin Nombre* 1, no. 4 (1971): 55–67.

Mendoza. María Luisa. "100 años de compañía." *El Día* (Mexico City), 21 July 1968.

Rodríguez Monegal, Emir. "Novedad y anacronismo en 'Cien años de soledad.'" *Revista Nacional de Cultura* 29, no. 185 (1968): 3–21.

⸺. "*One Hundred Years of Solitude:* The Last Three Pages." *Books Abroad* 47 (1973): 484–89.

Roldán de Micolta, Aleyda. "*Cien años de soledad:* una novela construida sobre espejos." *Explicación de Textos Literarios* 4, Suppl. 1 (1975–76): 239–57.

Rolfe, Doris. "Tono y estructura en *Cien años de soledad.*" *Explicación de Textos Literarios* 4, Suppl. 1 (1975–76): 259–82.

Salgado, María A. "¿'Civilización y barbarie' o 'Imaginación y barbarie'?" *Explicación de Textos Literarios* 4, Suppl. 1 (1975–76): 229–311.

Serra, Edelweis. "Narrema e isotopía en *Cien años de soledad.*" *Explicación de Textos Literarios* 4, Suppl. 1 (1975–76): 329–58.

Siemens, William L. "Tiempo, entropía y la estructura de *Cien años de soledad.*" *Explicación de Textos Literarios* 4, Suppl. 1 (1975–76): 359–71.

Vargas Llosa, Mario. *García Márquez: historia de un deicidio.* Barcelona: Monte Ávila Editores, 1971.

Sources on Guimarães Rosa's Work

Andrade, Vera Lúcia. "Conceituação de jugunço e jagunçagem em *Grande sertão: veredas.*" *Minas Gerais* (Lit. Suppl.) 28 May 1977, pp. 6–7.

Bueno, A. Sérgio. "A narrativa como caosmos: o medo e o amor em 'Grande sertão: veredas.'" *Minas Gerais* (Lit. Suppl.) 14 Feb. 1976, pp. 6–7.

Campos, Augusto de. "Um lance de 'dês' do grande sertão." *Minas Gerais* (Lit. Suppl) 30 Mar. 1974, pp. 4–7.

Cândido, Antônio. "O sertão e o mundo." *Minas Gerais* (Lit. Suppl.) 23 Mar. 1974, pp. 4–6.

Castro, Nei Leandro de. *Universo e vocabulário do grande sertão.* Rio de Janeiro: José Olympio, 1970.

Coelho, Nelly Novaes, and Ivana Versiani. *Guimarães Rosa: dois estudos.* São Paulo: Edições Quíron, 1975.

Daniel, Mary L. *João Guimarães Rosa: travessia literária.* Rio de Janeiro: José Olympio, 1968.

———. "Word Formation and Deformation in *Grande sertão: veredas.*" *Luso-Brazilian Review* 2 (1965): 81–97.

Faus, Francisco. "João Guimarães Rosa, le 'contemplatif transparent.'" *La Table Ronde* no. 195 (1964): 61–70.

Galvão, Walnice Nogueira. *As formas do falso: um estudo sobre a ambigüidade no* Grande sertão: veredas. São Paulo: Editora Perspectiva, 1972.

Garbuglio, José Carlos. *O mundo movente de Guimarães Rosa.* São Paulo: Editora Cultrix, 1972.

Lisboa, Henriqueta. "A poesia de *Grande sertão: veredas.*" *Revista do Livro* 3 (1958): 141–46.

Proença, M. Cavalcanti. "Alguns aspectos formais de *Grande sertão: veredas.*" *Minas Gerais* (Lit. Suppl.) 6 Apr. 1974, pp. 8–12.

Ramos, María Luísa. "O elemento poético em *Grande sertão: veredas.*" In *Ciclo de conferências sobre Guimarães Rosa,* pp. 53–75. Belo Horizonte: Centro de Estudos Mineiros, 1966.

Vincent, Jon S. *João Guimarães Rosa.* Boston: Twayne, 1978.

Xisto, Pedro. "À busca da poesia." In Pedro Xisto, Augusto de Campos, and Haroldo de Campos. *Guimarães Rosa em três dimensões,* pp. 7–39. São Paulo: Conselho Estadual de Cultura, n.d.

Index

Allegory, 15
Ambiguity: definition of, xii, 5–7, 26–28; increasing attention to, xii; importance in modern Latin American literature, xv; visual, 2–4, 19, 33, 60–61, 79, 95, 153; in music, 9; use of term, 9–11, 151; criteria of, 11; other phenomena contrasted with, 13–20; vagueness as a contributing factor to, 17–20; effects of, upon reader, 20–22, 152; as a unified sign, 21, 148–50, 154; and narrative structures, 26–28; deletion and, 29–30; system of clues in, 31; role of narrator in, 33–34, 43–45; as binder of motifs, 45–46; of story vs. expression, 74–82, 126–38; chiasmus and, 86; in sense of closure, 89–90; in repetition, 114–19; and jokes, 120–22, 153; in etymologies and morphology, 125–26; in art and life, 152–53; and acknowledgment of illusion, 153; and mysticism, 153. *See also* Disjunction, Mutually exclusives, Propositions
Assis, Machado de: an anachronism, xii; "O alienista," 16–17; critique of Eça de Queirós, 30. See also *Dom Casmurro*
Azevedo, Aluísio, 15
Azuela, Mariano, 15

Beardsley, Monroe, 30
Bernstein, Leonard, 9
Borges, Jorge Luis, 7–8

Chomsky, Noam, 23–24, 26–27
Chiasmus, 82–87
Cien años de soledad: ambiguous finality in, 89–90, 96–97; incompatibility of manuscript, storm and novel, 91–96;

compared with Penrose impossible object, 95–96; short circuit in, 95–96, 105–08; paradox in, 97, 106–07; criticism concerning ending of, 97–100; conservation of illusion in, 98–100, 112; mirrors in, 101, 123; readers in, 102–04; disconnection in, 108–09; self-destruction, self-reconstruction in, 109–11; abrupt reversals in, 111–12; conflicting perceptions in, 113–14; ambiguity of repetition in, 114–19; linearity vs. circularity in, 116–19; ambiguous joking in, 120–22; equivocal tone in, 122–24
Cohen, Jean, 136–39
Coleridge, Samuel Taylor, 93
Cortázar, Julio, 14, 17–18
Criticism: task of, xi, xiii; importance of ambiguity for, xii–xv; treatment of, on individual novels, xv–xvi; on *DC*, 14–15, 28–29; on *CAS*, 97–100; on *GSV*, 127–28, 131–36
Culler, Jonathan, xii–xv

Deautomatization, 20. *See also* Reader
Deconstruction, xiii–xv
Deletion, 29–30, 54–55. *See also* Vagueness
Derrida, Jacques, 19
Disjunction, 5–7, 8, 126, 140–50. *See also* Ambiguity
Dom Casmurro: polemic over, 14–15; deep and surface structures in, 25–26; narrative structures and ambiguity in, 26–28; Capitu's guilt or innocence of adultery in, 28–29, 31–43; deletion or gaps in, 29–31, 54–55; system of opposing clues in, 31–43; reliability of

183

Dom Casmurro (continued)
narrator in, 33–34, 43–45; bound and free motifs in, 45–46; metaphor in, 46–49, 51–55; pessimism in, 49–50; metalanguage in, 51–59; wave pattern in, 52–53; undertow and ambiguity in, 53–55; reader responses in, 55–59; centrality of ambiguity in, 63, 140

Echeverría, Esteban, 15
Eco, Umberto, 13
Empson, William, 10–11, 151
Ellis, Keith, 28

Fantastic, the, xii
Freedman, Ralph, 130
Freud, Sigmund, 120
Fuentes, Carlos, xv, 17

García Márquez, Gabriel. See *Cien años de soledad*
Gombrich, E. H., 100–01
Grande sertão: veredas: ambiguous etymologies in, 125–26; transparency vs. opacity of language in, 126–35, 138; stylistic devices in, 132–35; prose vs. poetry in, 130, 136–40; ambiguity as a thematic constant in, 141–45, 149–50; sound and semantic equivalence in, 141–42; intuitive evidence in, 145–46; layered contradictions in, 147–48; horizontal and vertical perception in, 149–50; mystical character of, 150

Hypotheses, finalized, xiv, 7, 12

Impossible objects, 2–3, 21–22, 95–96
Irony, 16

Jakobson, Roman, xii, 138–39

Kaplan, Abraham, 52
Kris, Ernst, 52

Leal, Luis, 63

Linguistic analogies in narrative theory, 23–28, 74–75
Lioret, E. Kent, 64
Logic, 5–7, 22, 43, 66, 105, 106

Meaning: determinacy/indeterminacy of, xiv–xv, 12, 13, 155–56; defined, 11–12; location of, 12
Metalanguage, xiii–xiv, 51–59, 101–14
Metaphor: contrasted with ambiguity, 15; in *DC*, 46–49, 51–55; in *GSV*, 141–42, 149–50
Motifs, free and bound, 45–46, 74
Music, ambiguity in, 9
Mutually exclusives, 5–7, 11, 80, 151, 155. See also Ambiguity

Narrative structures, deep and surface, 24–28, 63, 74, 78, 147
Narrator, reliability of, 33–34
New Criticism, Anglo-American, xii–xv

Open works, 13–14

Paradox: of self-referential ambiguity, xiv–xv, 124, 155; distinguished from ambiguity, 16–17; Cretan or liar, 17, 43–44, 97, 106–07, 155
Paz, Octavio, 14
Pedro Páramo: problem-solving mentality in, 60–62, 66–67; equivocation in, 61–62; Juan Preciado as prototype for reader in, 62, 87; relative stability of story, 63; pockets of ambiguity in, 63; 67; alive or dead in, 63–67; ambiguity surrounding Susana San Juan, 67–71; one or two Abundios in, 71–72; ambiguity of Páramo's death, 72–73; ordering or story vs. expression, 74–81; vs. *Los murmullos*, 79–81; disintegration and integration in, 81–82; chiasmus in, 82–87; doubles in, 86; definition of reader in, 87–88
Penrose, L. S. and R., 2–3, 9, 17

Plato, 98
Point of view, 43–45, 95
Poststructuralism, xii–xv
Propositions, exclusive, 8–9, 27, 31–32, 151. *See also* Ambiguity

Queirós, Eça de, 30

Ramos, Graciliano, 16
Reader: works encouraging participation of, 14; ambiguity's effects on, 20–22; problem-solving instinct of, 20, 60–61, 87; deautomatization in response of, 20; transcendence of the mundane in, 21; gap-filling capacity in, 30, 98–99, 104; responses of, in *DC*, 55–59, 154; prototype of, in *PP*, 62, 87–89, 154; suspension of disbelief in, 93, 112, 122; definitions of, in *CAS*, 101–04, 154; definition of, in *GSV*, 154; and natural images, 53–54, 154
Referentiality, xiv, 21–22
Representation vs. nonrepresentation, 9,

21–22, 79–80, 98–100, 126–40, 151–52
Rimmon, Shlomith, 5–7, 8, 11–12, 22, 27, 30, 94
Rodríguez Monegal, Emir, 116
Rosa, João Guimarães. See *Grande sertão: veredas*
Rubin, Edgar, 60–61, 79
Rulfo, Juan. See *Pedro Páramo*

Smith, Barbara Herrnstein, 89–90, 123
Structuralism, xii–xv
Symbolism, 15–16

Todorov, Tzvetan, xii
Tomashevsky, Boris, 45

Vagueness, 17–20. *See also* Deletion
Valéry, Paul, 9
Vargas Llosa, Mario, 107
Vincent, Jon S., 129

Winson, Elizabeth, 3–4, 8
Work of art, privileged status of, xi

ABOUT THE AUTHOR

Paul B. Dixon teaches Portuguese and Spanish at Purdue University. He received a bachelor of arts degree from Brigham Young University and a master of arts degree and doctorate from the University of North Carolina.